I0189878

Presence & Purpose:
50 Ways to Deepen Your Spiritual Self-Awareness

By Robert G. Jerus & Ronnie Cunningham
Published by Kaja Publishing
Paperback ISBN: 9798991745147

PUBLISHING

Copyright © 2025 By EIQ2 EI Center and Kaja Publishing, LLC. All rights reserved. No part of this publication may be reproduced, distributed, or transmitted in any form or by any means, including photocopying, recording, or other electronic or mechanical methods, without the prior written permission of the publisher, except in the case of brief quotations embodied in critical reviews and certain other noncommercial uses permitted by copyright law. For permission requests, email to the publisher at anton@kajapublishing.com.

Table of Contents

Introduction

Spiritual Awareness: The First 25 Ways

Self-Awareness

Introduction: An Invitation to Presence

Dear Fellow Traveler,

The book you hold in your hands began not in a moment of profound spiritual revelation, but in the ordinary struggles of my own journey—moments when God seemed distant, when emotions felt overwhelming, when the gap between what I believed and how I lived seemed impossibly wide. Perhaps you've found yourself in similar places, wondering how to bridge the distance between intellectual faith and lived experience, between knowing God exists and truly sensing His presence in your daily life.

I wrote these pages not as someone who has mastered spiritual awareness, but as a fellow pilgrim who continues to learn, stumble, grow, and discover. The 50 practices shared here have emerged from both ancient wisdom and contemporary understanding—the timeless truths of Scripture illuminated through the lens of emotional intelligence. They represent not a formula for perfect spirituality but a collection of pathways that have helped countless believers, including myself, move from religious routine to genuine relationship.

A Journey of Integration

For too long, many of us have been taught to separate our spiritual lives from our emotional experiences, as if feelings were somehow suspect or unspiritual. We've inherited approaches to faith that sometimes prioritize correct thinking over honest feeling, external behavior over internal transformation. Yet the God who created us designed us as integrated beings—our emotions, thoughts, bodies, and spirits working together to reflect His image.

At the EIQ2 EI Learning Center, we've witnessed the powerful intersection of emotional intelligence and spiritual formation. We've seen how understanding our emotions through a biblical lens creates pathways to deeper awareness of God's presence and clearer discernment of His purpose. The practices in this book reflect this integration—inviting you to engage not just your mind but your heart, not just your beliefs but your behaviors, not just your words but your whole being in the pursuit of God.

For Every Season of Faith

Some of you come to these pages in seasons of spiritual vitality, seeking to deepen what is already a meaningful connection with God. Others may be experiencing what feels like winter in your faith—a time of questioning, dryness, or distance. Still others stand at crossroads of significant transition, unsure of your next step but hungry for divine guidance. Some of you are spiritual leaders, carrying not only your own journey but responsibility for guiding others.

Wherever you find yourself, know that these pages offer not judgment but invitation. Each practice is a doorway, not a demand—an opportunity to experience God's presence more fully rather than another spiritual obligation to fulfill. You need not implement all fifty at once; even one practice embraced wholeheartedly can become a channel through which living water begins to flow into parched places.

How to Use This Book

The structure of this book is intentionally simple. Each practice includes a clear concept, a supporting scripture, an explanation that bridges theological understanding with practical application, and an elaboration that connects the practice to daily life. You might choose to:

- Read through the entire book first to gain an overview, then return to specific practices that resonate most deeply
- Focus on one practice each week, allowing seven days to explore and implement it before moving to the next
- Use the book as a reference, turning to particular practices that address your current spiritual needs
- Share the journey with others, perhaps in a small group where you can discuss your experiences and insights

There is no wrong approach except the one that turns these invitations into burdens. Jesus came that we might have life abundantly, not that we might have longer spiritual to-do lists.

An Ongoing Conversation

My deepest hope is that these pages become not just another book you've read but a conversation partner in your spiritual journey—a companion that walks alongside you, offering both challenge and comfort as you pursue greater awareness of God's presence and purpose in your life. The practices in this book are simply ways of positioning yourself to receive what He already freely offers: His presence, which is our ultimate purpose. As you turn these pages, may you discover not just information about God but transformation through encounter with Him. And may you experience the truth that has sustained believers through centuries of challenge and change: that God is nearer than we think, more loving than we dare hope, and more committed to our growth than we can imagine.

The journey awaits. Shall we begin?

With faith, hope, and love,

Robert G. Jerus

EIQ2 EI Center

Spiritual Awareness: The First 25 Ways

Spiritual awareness is the conscious recognition of God's presence and purpose in our daily lives—a state of being where we not only acknowledge His existence but actively engage with Him through prayer, Scripture, and mindful attention to His movement in our world. It's about developing spiritual sight that sees beyond the physical realm into the deeper workings of God's kingdom, allowing us to live with intention and divine perspective.

Many believers struggle with feeling disconnected from God despite their sincere faith. In our fast-paced, distraction-filled world, spiritual numbness can settle in, leaving us wondering why our relationship with God feels distant or mechanical. Others battle persistent anxiety, finding it difficult to experience the peace that Scripture promises, even when they intellectually know God's truths. Developing spiritual awareness brings great joy as we experience God's presence in tangible ways. There's an incomparable delight in recognizing His fingerprints in unexpected moments—whether through a timely word from a friend, a passage of Scripture that suddenly illuminates your situation, or a moment of clarity during prayer. This awareness transforms ordinary days into sacred journeys of discovery, where even routine tasks become opportunities for connection with the divine. The deep sense of belonging that comes from knowing you're walking in step with your Creator provides a foundation of joy that circumstances cannot easily shake.

Spiritual awareness doesn't require theological expertise or extraordinary spiritual gifts—it begins with simple practices accessible to every believer. Starting with just five minutes of intentional silence each day can create space for God's voice to become more recognizable. The magic of spiritual awareness is that it builds upon itself—each moment of recognition trains your spiritual senses to become more attuned to God's presence and voice. Scripture repeatedly emphasizes the importance of spiritual awareness, from David's passionate desire to "dwell in the house of the Lord all the days of my life, to gaze upon the beauty of the Lord" (Psalm 27:4) to Paul's encouragement to "pray without ceasing" (1 Thessalonians 5:17). Jesus himself modeled spiritual awareness by consistently withdrawing to quiet places for communion with the Father, demonstrating that connection with God is the wellspring from which all meaningful ministry flows. The Bible presents spiritual awareness not as an optional upgrade to our faith but as the essential foundation for a life that bears lasting fruit.

At the EIQ2 EI Learning Center, we understand that emotional intelligence and spiritual awareness are intrinsically connected—both involving self-awareness, intentional response rather than reaction, and meaningful engagement with others. The following 25 ways to deepen your spiritual awareness incorporate principles of emotional intelligence viewed through a biblical lens, offering practical steps toward a more vibrant, present, and purposeful faith journey. Each concept builds upon the understanding that we are created in God's image—including our emotional capacity—and that growing in awareness of His presence transforms both our relationship with Him and our emotional landscape.

1. Meditate

Focus your mind and heart on spiritual truths and biblical teachings to gain deeper insights and foster a closer relationship with God. This simple practice of focusing your mind and heart on spiritual truths and biblical teachings creates a key foundation for spiritual growth. When you intentionally direct your attention to these sacred wisdom sources, you open yourself to revelations that might otherwise remain hidden beneath the noise of daily life. This deliberate contemplation allows God's word to penetrate beyond intellectual understanding, touching the deeper chambers of your heart where true transformation occurs. As you regularly engage with these teachings, you develop spiritual discernment that helps you recognize God's presence and guidance in your everyday experiences. This practice doesn't just increase your knowledge about faith—it fundamentally shifts how you perceive yourself and the world around you, cultivating a more intimate connection with God and a heightened awareness of His work in your life.

Joshua 1:8 - "Keep this Book of the Law always on your lips; meditate on it day and night, so that you may be careful to do everything written in it. Then you will be prosperous and successful."

Biblical meditation stands in stark contrast to the emptying of the mind practiced in some Eastern traditions. Instead, it involves the intentional filling of our minds with God's Word and truth. This practice invites us to slow down, to carefully consider each word and phrase of Scripture, allowing its wisdom to penetrate beyond mere intellectual understanding into our hearts and actions. Meditation creates space for the Holy Spirit to illuminate God's Word in fresh ways, making ancient truths personally relevant and transformative.

When God commissioned Joshua to lead Israel after Moses' death, He didn't primarily emphasize strategic military plans or leadership techniques. Instead, He highlighted meditation on Scripture as the foundation for Joshua's success. This divine instruction reveals a profound truth: our effectiveness in fulfilling God's purposes flows directly from our internalization of His Word. The promise attached to this practice—prosperity and success—isn't primarily about material wealth but about flourishing in God's purposes and succeeding in what truly matters. As we meditate on Scripture day and night, allowing it to be "always on our lips," we develop spiritual awareness that shapes our decisions, redirects our desires, and transforms our identity, equipping us to navigate life's challenges with divine wisdom and perspective.

2. Pray

Communicate with God to express gratitude, seek guidance, and strengthen your faith and reliance on Him. Establishing a consistent prayer practice creates a vital channel of communication with God that nurtures your spiritual life from its very roots. When you pray—whether through formal devotions or spontaneous conversations—you're actively acknowledging God's presence and sovereignty in your life. This sacred dialogue allows you to pour out your gratitude, concerns, and deepest yearnings while creating space to receive divine wisdom and direction. Through prayer, you develop spiritual muscles that help you navigate life's challenges with greater resilience and discernment. More than a religious obligation, prayer becomes the heartbeat of an authentic relationship with God, gradually transforming how you perceive life's circumstances and deepening your awareness of God's constant companionship. As you practice vulnerability and honesty in prayer, you'll find your faith strengthened and your spiritual awareness heightened in ways that extend far beyond the moments spent in devotion.

1 Thessalonians 5:17 - "Pray continually."

Prayer is the heartbeat of spiritual awareness—the ongoing conversation that keeps us connected to God throughout our daily lives. Far more than a religious obligation or a wish list presented to a distant deity, prayer is intimate communion with the Creator who knows us completely and loves us perfectly. This sacred dialogue invites us to bring our authentic selves—our joys and sorrows, certainties and doubts, strengths and weaknesses—before the One who designed us and desires a relationship with us.

Paul's succinct command to "pray continually" might initially seem impossible in our busy lives, but this instruction isn't about maintaining uninterrupted verbal prayer. Rather, it describes a state of ongoing spiritual attentiveness—a constant awareness of God's presence that transforms ordinary moments into opportunities for connection. This continuous prayer becomes possible when we recognize that prayer isn't limited to formal, eyes-closed sessions but encompasses every genuine turning of our hearts toward God: the whispered "thank you" for a moment of beauty, the silent plea for patience during a challenging interaction, the wordless sigh of dependence when facing uncertainty. As we practice this continual conversation, we develop an emotional intelligence that recognizes God's movements in our lives, allowing His peace to stabilize our emotions, His wisdom to guide our decisions, and His love to shape our interactions with others.

3. Have Reflective Quiet Time

Dedicate time to be alone with God, reflecting on His word and your life, which allows for spiritual renewal and clarity. Carving out intentional quiet time with God serves as a spiritual reset button in our increasingly chaotic world. During these sacred moments of solitude, the constant background noise of life fades away, creating space for divine wisdom to emerge with remarkable clarity. This practice allows Scripture to sink deeper into your consciousness as you thoughtfully consider how God's timeless truths apply to your specific circumstances. The reflective nature of this discipline helps you recognize patterns in your spiritual journey, discern God's guidance more clearly, and gain perspective on challenges that might otherwise overwhelm you. As you consistently prioritize these intimate encounters with God, you'll discover a growing spiritual sensitivity that transforms how you navigate each day. This quiet communion becomes a wellspring of renewal, gradually reshaping your awareness of God's presence and cultivating a deeper spiritual intuition that remains with you long after your designated quiet time has ended.

Mark 1:35 - "Very early in the morning, while it was still dark, Jesus got up, left the house and went off to a solitary place, where he prayed."

In the midst of our hyper-connected world with its constant notifications and endless distractions, intentional solitude has become both increasingly rare and profoundly necessary. Reflective quiet time carves out a sanctuary in our overscheduled lives—a sacred space where we can temporarily set aside the voices and demands of others to hear the still, small voice of God. This practice isn't about escaping responsibility but about gaining the perspective and spiritual nourishment needed to fulfill our responsibilities with wisdom and grace.

Jesus himself, despite the pressing demands of his ministry and the constant needs of the crowds, prioritized these moments of solitary communion with the Father. The Gospel of Mark reveals that even after a long evening of healing the sick, Jesus rose before dawn to seek this essential connection. If the Son of God—who possessed perfect communion with the Father—recognized his need for dedicated quiet time, how much more do we require these intentional pauses? By following Christ's example of deliberate withdrawal, we acknowledge our dependence on God and create the conditions for spiritual renewal. These moments of reflection allow us to process our emotions honestly before God, examine our motivations, realign our priorities with divine purposes, and receive the clarity and strength needed for the day ahead. In the silence, we often discover that God has been speaking all along—we simply needed to create the space to listen.

4. Study and Contemplate

Explore deeply into the scriptures to understand God's teachings and how they apply to your life. Intentional scripture study and contemplation serve as transformative gateways to spiritual revelation and personal growth. When you move beyond casual reading to truly investigate biblical teachings, you uncover layers of meaning that speak directly to your unique circumstances and questions. This deliberate exploration creates space for the Holy Spirit to illuminate connections between ancient wisdom and contemporary challenges, bringing scripture to life in remarkably personal ways. Through thoughtful study, you develop spiritual discernment that helps you distinguish between cultural influences and eternal truths, allowing God's perspective to reshape your values and priorities. As you consistently engage in this practice, scripture gradually becomes less of an external reference and more of an internal compass, deeply informing your decisions and reactions. This contemplative approach to God's word nurtures a rich spiritual awareness that transforms not just what you know intellectually, but how you perceive yourself, others, and God's ongoing work in the world around you.

Acts 17:11 - "Now the Berean Jews were of more noble character than those in Thessalonica, for they received the message with great eagerness and examined the Scriptures every day to see if what Paul said was true."

Biblical study involves more than casual reading—it requires deliberate investigation, thoughtful analysis, and persistent questioning that leads to genuine understanding. This intellectual engagement with Scripture honors God by taking His Word seriously enough to invest time and mental energy in comprehending its meaning. While meditation often focuses on absorbing and internalizing smaller portions of text, study expands our vision to see how individual passages connect to the broader biblical narrative and theological framework, providing essential context that protects us from misinterpretation.

The Bereans exemplify this approach to Scripture, earning Luke's commendation as "more noble" because of their disciplined study habits. What distinguished these believers wasn't skepticism but rather a commitment to verifying every teaching against the authoritative Word of God—even when the teacher was the apostle Paul himself. Their example challenges us to develop a healthy biblical discernment that weighs all spiritual claims against Scripture. When we approach Bible study with both the Bereans' "great eagerness" and their careful examination, we develop an emotional intelligence that distinguishes between truth and error, substance and superficiality. This disciplined contemplation transforms our thinking patterns, equipping us to apply biblical principles to complex situations, recognize God's perspective on contemporary issues, and articulate our faith with clarity and conviction. In a world of competing voices and conflicting viewpoints, deep scriptural knowledge becomes an anchor for our spiritual awareness, keeping us grounded in God's unchanging truth.

5. Be Mindful of God

Keep God's presence and His will at the forefront of your mind throughout your daily activities. Developing a continuous awareness of God's presence transforms ordinary moments into sacred encounters with the divine. When you intentionally practice God-consciousness throughout your day—whether in meetings, family interactions, or solitary tasks—you begin to recognize His guiding hand in circumstances you might otherwise dismiss as coincidental or mundane. This ongoing spiritual mindfulness gradually reorients your perspective, helping you filter decisions, conversations, and reactions through the lens of God's will rather than merely personal preference or cultural pressure. As this practice deepens, you'll find yourself developing spiritual reflexes that respond to challenges with greater wisdom and peace, even before conscious thought intervenes. This constant communion with God softens the artificial boundary between "spiritual activities" and "everyday life," allowing your faith to permeate all aspects of your existence. By keeping God at the forefront of your consciousness, you create space for continuous spiritual growth and a more authentic alignment between your outward actions and your inner spiritual identity.

Proverbs 3:6 - "In all your ways acknowledge Him, and He will make your paths straight."

Mindfulness of God transforms ordinary moments into sacred encounters and routine decisions into opportunities for obedience. This awareness isn't limited to traditionally "spiritual" activities but extends to every aspect of life—our work and rest, our conversations and entertainment choices, our spending habits and relationship dynamics. Being mindful of God means recognizing His relevance in contexts where we might otherwise operate on autopilot, guided solely by habit, convenience, or conventional wisdom. It's about developing a spiritual sensitivity that asks, "How does God's perspective apply here?" in situations ranging from major life choices to seemingly insignificant daily interactions.

The promise in Proverbs 3:6 reveals that acknowledging God "in all your ways" leads to straight paths—not necessarily easier journeys, but clearer direction and purposeful progress. The Hebrew word for "acknowledge" (yada) implies more than intellectual recognition; it suggests intimate knowing and intentional inclusion. When we practice this comprehensive acknowledgment of God, inviting His presence into each dimension of our lives, we experience His guidance in practical ways: clarity in decision-making, wisdom in relationships, discernment in opportunities, and protection from detours that waste time and energy. This mindfulness doesn't demand dramatic changes to our daily routines but rather a reorientation of awareness that infuses familiar activities with sacred significance. Whether preparing a meal, engaging in a business meeting, or enjoying recreation, the practice of God-mindfulness elevates ordinary experiences into worship, transforming not just what we do but how we experience what we do.

6. Journalize

Write down your thoughts, prayers, and spiritual insights to track your growth and remember God's faithfulness. The practice of spiritual journaling creates a tangible record of your faith journey that serves as both mirror and memorial in your walk with God. When you document your prayers, questions, and moments of insight, you're establishing sacred landmarks that help you recognize patterns of divine activity in your life that might otherwise go unnoticed. This written reflection becomes a powerful testimony to God's faithfulness during challenging seasons, providing concrete evidence of spiritual growth when progress feels imperceptible. The act of journaling also clarifies your thoughts, often revealing deeper truths as your pen moves across the page—insights that might remain nebulous if left unexplored. Over time, this collection of spiritual reflections becomes a personal sacred text that chronicles your unique relationship with God, offering encouragement during spiritual droughts and cultivating a richer awareness of how the divine intersects with your daily experience. Through this intentional practice, you develop a more discerning spiritual eye that sees God's handiwork not just in dramatic moments but in the subtle unfolding of your everyday life.

Psalm 102:18 - "Let this be written for a future generation, that a people not yet created may praise the LORD."

Spiritual journaling creates a tangible record of our walk with God—documenting our questions and insights, struggles and victories, prayers and their answers. This practice transforms fleeting thoughts into permanent reflections that can be revisited, allowing us to recognize patterns in our spiritual journey and witness God's consistent faithfulness over time. The act of writing itself often brings clarity, helping us process complex emotions, articulate vague spiritual impressions, and identify the subtle movements of God that might otherwise go unnoticed in the rush of daily life.

The psalmist's words reveal the profound impact that documented spiritual experiences can have—not just on our own faith but potentially on generations to come. When we record God's work in our lives, we create a legacy of faith that testifies to His character and actions. This doesn't mean our journals need to be literary masterpieces or theological treatises; simple, honest accounts of our spiritual journey can become powerful testimonies. Whether through traditional handwritten journals, digital notes, artistic expressions, or audio recordings, the practice of documenting our spiritual journey serves both as an act of worship and a monument to God's faithfulness. In moments of doubt or spiritual dryness, these recorded testimonies become tangible reminders of God's past work, encouraging us to trust His continued presence and activity in our lives.

7. Seek Wisdom

Actively pursue God's wisdom, which is key to living a righteous and fulfilling life. The deliberate pursuit of divine wisdom fundamentally transforms how you navigate life's complex situations. Unlike worldly knowledge that merely informs, godly wisdom illuminates your path with discernment that aligns your choices with eternal values rather than temporary desires. When you actively seek this higher understanding—through scripture, prayer, and spiritual community—you develop spiritual vision that sees beyond immediate circumstances to recognize the deeper currents of God's activity in your life. This wisdom-seeking journey gradually refines your spiritual intuition, helping you distinguish between cultural voices and divine guidance even in ambiguous situations. As this heavenly perspective takes root in your heart, it reshapes not just your decisions but your very desires, bringing them into greater harmony with God's purposes. The faithful pursuit of wisdom creates a foundation for authentic spiritual awareness that transforms your relationships, priorities, and responses to life's challenges, allowing you to experience the profound fulfillment that comes from living in alignment with God's design for your life.

James 1:5 - "If any of you lacks wisdom, you should ask God, who gives generously to all without finding fault, and it will be given to you."

Divine wisdom transcends mere intellectual knowledge or accumulated information—it's the practical discernment that enables us to navigate life's complexities according to God's principles. Unlike worldly wisdom, which often prioritizes self-advancement and immediate gratification, godly wisdom seeks to align our choices with eternal values and God's redemptive purposes. This wisdom manifests in our ability to distinguish between truth and deception, to recognize the long-term consequences of present decisions, and to respond to challenges with both conviction and compassion.

James offers extraordinary encouragement for those who recognize their need for this wisdom, presenting God as a generous giver who delights in granting this gift "without finding fault." This promise assures us that God doesn't withhold wisdom because of our past failures or current shortcomings; He doesn't respond to our requests with criticism about why we didn't seek wisdom earlier or in other situations. Instead, He gives liberally to all who ask in faith. This divine generosity invites us to approach God confidently with our need for discernment in specific circumstances—whether facing ethical dilemmas at work, navigating relationship challenges, making stewardship decisions, or determining ministry directions. As we consistently seek His wisdom through prayer, Scripture, godly counsel, and attentiveness to the Holy Spirit's guidance, we develop spiritual awareness that recognizes His voice more clearly and reflects His perspective more accurately in our daily choices.

8. Serve/Share and be a Good Steward

Use your talents and resources to serve others and glorify God, managing all He has entrusted to you with care. The practice of generous stewardship creates a powerful spiritual feedback loop that deepens your awareness of God's presence in every aspect of life. When you intentionally view your talents, time, and resources as divine gifts rather than personal possessions, you begin operating from a fundamentally different spiritual perspective. This mindset shift transforms ordinary acts of service into sacred opportunities for worship, allowing you to experience God's character more intimately through your own acts of giving. As you faithfully manage what has been entrusted to you—whether material resources or intangible gifts—you develop a heightened sensitivity to God's provision and purposes in your life. This stewardship journey gradually reshapes your spiritual awareness, helping you recognize divine appointments and opportunities that might otherwise be missed. The practice of serving others from this place of grateful responsibility creates tangible expressions of your faith that authenticate your spiritual journey, both to yourself and to those around you, cultivating a richly textured spiritual awareness that connects your internal beliefs with external actions in ways that honor God and reflect His nature to the world.

1 Peter 4:10 - "Each of you should use whatever gift you have received to serve others, as faithful stewards of God's grace in its various forms."

Stewardship extends far beyond financial management to encompass every resource God has placed in our care—our time and talents, relationships and influence, opportunities and spiritual gifts. This perspective transforms how we view our possessions and abilities, recognizing them not as personal achievements to be hoarded but as divine provisions to be invested for Kingdom purposes. True stewardship flows from the understanding that everything we have ultimately belongs to God, and we are temporary managers rather than permanent owners.

Peter's instruction highlights both the diversity of gifts within the body of Christ and the unified purpose they serve. The phrase "God's grace in its various forms" acknowledges that spiritual gifts manifest differently in each believer, yet all originate from the same divine grace. Whether our gifts are visible or behind-the-scenes, whether they involve speaking or serving, leadership or support, each has been divinely distributed for the common good. When we steward these gifts faithfully, we participate in the remarkable economy of God's kingdom, where nothing is wasted and every contribution matters. This service-oriented approach to stewardship creates a heightened spiritual awareness that recognizes opportunities to invest our resources in eternal purposes—seeing needs through God's eyes, hearing requests with God's ears, and responding with hands and hearts aligned with God's generous character. As we faithfully manage what God has entrusted to us, we experience the paradoxical truth that we find greater fulfillment in giving than in keeping, and we discover that our resources multiply rather than diminish when shared in service to others.

9. Be Grateful

Cultivate an attitude of gratitude towards God for all His blessings, recognizing His goodness in all things. The practice of intentional gratitude fundamentally recalibrates your spiritual awareness, creating a powerful lens through which God's presence becomes more visible in everyday moments. When you deliberately cultivate thankfulness—even during challenging seasons—you're developing spiritual muscles that recognize divine fingerprints in circumstances that might otherwise seem ordinary or difficult. This grateful perspective gradually transforms how you process life experiences, shifting your focus from what's lacking to the abundant evidence of God's faithfulness surrounding you. As this practice deepens, gratitude becomes less of an occasional response and more of a spiritual posture from which you naturally operate, allowing you to perceive blessings that might otherwise go unnoticed in the rush of daily life. The habit of thankfulness creates a sacred space where spiritual insights flourish, helping you recognize the intricate ways God is working in and through your circumstances. Through consistent grateful acknowledgment, your spiritual perception sharpens, enabling you to experience a richer communion with God and a more profound awareness of His constant goodness threading through every aspect of your journey.

1 Thessalonians 5:18 - "Give thanks in all circumstances; for this is God's will for you in Christ Jesus."

Gratitude is the antidote to many spiritual and emotional ailments—it counters entitlement with appreciation, transforms complaint into praise, and shifts our focus from what we lack to the abundance we've received. This practice isn't about denying difficulties or suppressing negative emotions, but rather about developing spiritual vision that can recognize God's goodness even in challenging seasons. Genuine gratitude acknowledges both the obvious blessings that everyone can see and the hidden mercies that require more discerning eyes to recognize.

Paul's instruction to "give thanks in all circumstances" presents one of the most challenging yet transformative spiritual disciplines. Note that he doesn't command thanksgiving for all circumstances, but in all circumstances—a crucial distinction that acknowledges the reality of suffering while affirming that gratitude remains possible even amid pain. This command is immediately followed by the assurance that such comprehensive thanksgiving fulfills "God's will for you in Christ Jesus," suggesting that gratitude isn't merely a positive psychological practice but a spiritual posture that aligns us with divine purposes. When we intentionally practice thanksgiving—whether through spoken prayers, written lists, or deliberate pauses to acknowledge God's gifts—we develop emotional intelligence that resists both entitled expectation and bitter resentment. This grateful awareness becomes spiritually formative, training our hearts to recognize God's faithful provision, protection, and presence in every season of life. As we consistently give thanks, we discover that gratitude isn't just our response to blessing but often becomes the very pathway to experiencing deeper blessing.

10. Encourage Kindness & Compassion

Reflect God's love through acts of kindness and compassion towards others, demonstrating the character of Christ. Practicing deliberate kindness and compassion creates a powerful spiritual conduit through which God's character flows tangibly into a broken world. When you choose to respond with gentle understanding rather than judgment, or offer help without expectation of return, you're participating in a sacred reflection of divine love that transcends religious routine. These compassionate actions become living prayers that align your heart more closely with God's, developing spiritual sensitivity that recognizes the divine image in every person you encounter. As this practice deepens, you begin experiencing profound moments of spiritual awareness in ordinary interactions—glimpsing God's presence in the grateful smile of someone you've helped or feeling His pleasure in your decision to extend grace when it wasn't deserved. The consistent practice of Christ-like compassion gradually transforms your spiritual perception, helping you recognize divine appointments amid everyday encounters and cultivating a heightened awareness of how God is using your simple acts of kindness as instruments of His healing presence in places where formal ministry might never reach.

Colossians 3:12 - "Therefore, as God's chosen people, holy and dearly loved, clothe yourselves with compassion, kindness, humility, gentleness and patience."

Kindness and compassion are not merely nice additions to our character but essential expressions of our identity as God's beloved children. These qualities move beyond occasional charitable acts to become consistent patterns that shape how we perceive and respond to others. True compassion enables us to see beyond surface behaviors to the underlying needs, wounds, and struggles of those around us, while kindness translates that empathetic insight into tangible action. Together, these attributes form a powerful witness to Christ's presence in our lives, making the abstract concept of God's love concrete and visible.

Paul's metaphor of "clothing ourselves" with these virtues suggests an intentional daily choice—just as we deliberately select our physical garments each morning, we must consciously put on these spiritual qualities. The foundation for this choice lies in our identity as those who are "holy and dearly loved," indicating that our compassionate treatment of others flows from our secure experience of God's love for us. When we truly grasp how deeply we are loved despite our flaws, we become more capable of extending that same grace-filled perspective to others. This spiritual awareness transforms ordinary interactions—listening attentively to someone who needs to talk, offering encouragement during a colleague's difficult day, responding with patience to a child's repeated questions, or showing practical help to a neighbor in need. As we consistently practice these Christlike responses, we participate in God's redemptive work, creating spaces where others can experience His character through our actions. In a world often marked by harshness and indifference, such kindness and compassion stand out as powerful testimonies to the transformative reality of God's kingdom.

11. Be Merciful/Forgive; Be Graceful

Embrace mercy and forgiveness in your interactions, reflecting God's grace in your life towards others. Forgiveness and mercy represent transformative expressions of God's character in our lives—they allow us to release the burden of resentment while offering others the same grace we've received. This practice doesn't minimize wrongdoing or eliminate appropriate boundaries, but rather frees us from the prison of bitterness that damages our own spiritual health. When we choose forgiveness, we mirror the divine mercy that forms the foundation of our relationship with God, creating potential for healing in even the most wounded relationships.

Ephesians 4:32 - "Be kind and compassionate to one another, forgiving each other, just as in Christ God forgave you."

Forgiveness and mercy represent some of the most challenging yet transformative aspects of Christian character—they require us to release our legitimate claim to justice or retribution and instead offer undeserved kindness. This gracious response doesn't minimize or excuse wrongdoing, but rather chooses to break the cycle of hurt by refusing to let another's actions determine our response. When we extend forgiveness, we liberate not only the offender from the weight of guilt but also ourselves from the burden of resentment and bitterness that can poison our spiritual and emotional well-being.

Paul's instruction anchors our forgiveness of others in our own experience of divine forgiveness—"just as in Christ God forgave you." This comparison establishes both the motivation and the measure for our mercy toward others. When we truly comprehend the magnitude of what we've been forgiven—the depth of our sin and the tremendous cost of Christ's sacrifice—our reluctance to forgive others is confronted with a powerful perspective. God's forgiveness of us wasn't grudging, partial, or contingent on our worthiness, but rather complete, costly, and offered while we were still His enemies. This divine example challenges us to extend grace even when it feels unnatural or undeserved. As we practice this mercy-filled approach to relationships, we develop spiritual awareness that recognizes opportunities for reconciliation where others see only irreparable division. Each act of forgiveness becomes not only a reflection of God's character but also a participation in His ongoing work of restoration, creating spaces where broken relationships can be healed and renewed through the same grace that has transformed our own lives.

12. Be Generous and Giving

Cultivate a spirit of generosity, sharing your resources and blessings with others as a reflection of God's generosity towards you. The practice of intentional generosity opens spiritual windows that reveal God's abundant nature working through your everyday choices. When you freely give—whether through financial resources, time, or talents—you're engaging in a profound spiritual exercise that mirrors God's own giving character, creating a deeper connection with His heart. This willing release of what you possess challenges the soul's natural tendency toward self-protection, gradually transforming your spiritual awareness from scarcity thinking to recognizing divine provision flowing through your life rather than simply to you. As this generous mindset becomes more ingrained, you'll begin noticing sacred opportunities for giving that might previously have gone unrecognized, developing spiritual discernment that sees needs through God's compassionate perspective. The joy that accompanies authentic generosity serves as a tangible reminder of God's presence, affirming that you're participating in His divine economy rather than merely following religious obligation. Through consistent giving, your spiritual sensitivity expands beyond personal blessings to encompass a richer awareness of your role as a conduit of God's generosity in a world desperate for evidence of His goodness.

2 Corinthians 9:7 - "Each of you should give what you have decided in your heart to give, not reluctantly or under compulsion, for God loves a cheerful giver."

Generosity extends far beyond financial donations to encompass a whole-life orientation of open-handed living. This spiritual posture recognizes that everything we have—our time, talents, possessions, and opportunities—comes ultimately from God's provision and is entrusted to us not just for personal benefit but for kingdom purposes. True generosity flows from gratitude rather than guilt, from delight rather than duty, transforming giving from an obligation we fulfill to an opportunity we embrace.

Paul's guidance on giving emphasizes both thoughtful intention ("what you have decided in your heart") and joyful attitude ("cheerful giver"), revealing that the spirit behind our giving matters as much to God as the gift itself. The Greek word translated as "cheerful" (hilaros, from which we get our English word "hilarious") suggests not just absence of reluctance but actual delight in the act of giving. This cheerfulness doesn't require wealth or abundance—some of the most joyful givers are those with limited resources who nonetheless share generously from what they have. God's preference for this cheerful giving reminds us that generosity is meant to be liberating rather than burdensome, an expression of trust rather than a transaction. As we practice intentional generosity, we develop spiritual awareness that sees our resources through God's perspective—recognizing opportunities to invest in eternal purposes rather than merely accumulating temporal possessions. Each generous act becomes both worship of a generous God and witness to His kingdom values, creating ripples of blessing that extend far beyond the immediate gift.

13. Help Others/Contribute

Actively seek opportunities to assist others, contributing to their well-being as an expression of God's love and compassion. The deliberate practice of helping others creates sacred intersections where your faith becomes tangibly expressed through meaningful action. When you intentionally seek opportunities to meet needs—whether through significant contributions or small daily kindnesses—you're participating in a divine extension of God's compassionate presence in the world. This outward focus gradually refines your spiritual vision, helping you recognize needs you might otherwise overlook and discern specific ways your unique gifts can address them. As you consistently serve others without expectation of recognition or return, you often experience unexpected moments of spiritual clarity and connection with God that transcend what's typically found in more traditional spiritual disciplines. This helping mindset creates a beautiful paradox where giving becomes receiving—not of material benefit, but of deepened spiritual awareness as you glimpse God's heart for those you serve. Through faithful contribution to others' wellbeing, your understanding of faith evolves from abstract belief to lived experience, cultivating a rich spiritual sensitivity that recognizes divine appointments in everyday encounters and experiences God's presence most profoundly in moments of selfless service.

Hebrews 13:16 - "And do not forget to do good and to share with others, for with such sacrifices God is pleased."

Helping others transforms abstract spiritual principles into tangible expressions of faith. This practice invites us to move beyond theoretical compassion to practical action—addressing real needs, alleviating genuine suffering, and providing substantive support to those around us. When we intentionally contribute to others' well-being, we participate in God's redemptive work, becoming channels of divine care in a broken world. This assistance might take countless forms: offering practical help to a neighbor, mentoring someone in need of guidance, providing resources during a crisis, or simply being present with someone during a difficult season.

The writer of Hebrews frames this help and sharing as "sacrifices" that please God, suggesting that meaningful contribution often involves personal cost—whether of time, comfort, convenience, or resources. This sacrificial element distinguishes genuine helping from token gestures, requiring us to give in ways that we actually feel. Yet paradoxically, these sacrifices that cost us something become sources of deep fulfillment, aligning us with God's heart for humanity. The exhortation "do not forget" acknowledges our tendency to become absorbed in our own concerns and inadvertently overlook opportunities to help others. This reminder calls us to cultivated attentiveness—a spiritual awareness that notices needs we might otherwise miss and responds with practical compassion. As we consistently practice this outward-focused living, we discover that helping others isn't an interruption to our spiritual life but rather a central expression of it—a way of embodying the love we've received and participating in God's ongoing work of restoration and redemption in our communities.

14. Trust in the Lord/Believe in His Promises

Place your faith and trust in God, relying on His promises and faithfulness in all circumstances. Develop unwavering trust in God's promises creates a spiritual foundation that remains steady even when circumstances seem to contradict divine goodness. When you deliberately choose faith over fear—especially during seasons of uncertainty or waiting—you're engaging in a profound spiritual practice that gradually transforms your perception of life's challenges. This trust journey develops spiritual muscles that recognize God's faithful hand working behind seemingly random events, allowing you to respond to difficulties with a peace that transcends mere positive thinking. As this trust deepens, you'll notice a shift in your spiritual awareness from anxious scanning of circumstances to a settled confidence in God's character that remains unshaken by external pressures. The practice of actively believing God's promises recalibrates your spiritual sensitivity, helping you detect divine activity in situations where others might see only coincidence or misfortune. Through consistent trust in God's faithfulness, you develop a spiritually attuned heart that perceives the intricate ways He is fulfilling His word in your life, often in ways more beautiful and complex than your limited understanding could have anticipated.

Proverbs 3:5-6 - *"Trust in the Lord with all your heart and lean not on your own understanding; in all your ways submit to him, and he will make your paths straight."*

Trust in God represents the foundational posture of authentic faith—the deliberate choice to rely on God's character, wisdom, and faithfulness rather than our limited perspective. This trust isn't blind optimism or passive resignation but a confident dependence based on who God has revealed Himself to be. When we trust God, we acknowledge both our limitations and His limitlessness, recognizing that our understanding—however informed or intelligent—remains partial and imperfect compared to His comprehensive wisdom.

Solomon's instruction in Proverbs presents this trust as comprehensive ("with all your heart"), contrasting it with self-reliance ("lean not on your own understanding"). The Hebrew concept of "heart" encompasses not just emotions but also mind, will, and the core of our being, suggesting that trust must permeate every dimension of our lives. The promise attached to this trust—straight paths—doesn't guarantee absence of obstacles but rather assures divine guidance and purposeful direction. This guidance comes as we "submit to him in all our ways," aligning our choices with His values and surrendering our plans to His purposes. Trusting God in this comprehensive manner develops spiritual awareness that recognizes His sovereignty in every circumstance— seeing opportunities where others see only obstacles, finding peace amid uncertainty, and maintaining hope during apparent setbacks. Rather than being a one-time decision, this trust becomes a moment-by-moment choice to view our circumstances through the lens of God's character and promises, allowing His perfect perspective to override our natural tendency toward anxiety, control, or despair.

15. Obey Scripture

Live according to God's Word, following His commands and teachings as the foundation of your spiritual life. Scripture-based obedience creates a transformative spiritual framework that anchors your faith in action rather than mere intellectual agreement. When you intentionally align your choices with biblical teachings—even when they challenge cultural norms or personal desires—you're creating space for profound spiritual growth that cannot be achieved through knowledge alone. This lived commitment to God's word gradually refines your spiritual discernment, developing an inner sensitivity that recognizes divine guidance with increasing clarity. As this obedient posture becomes more habitual, you'll begin experiencing scripture not as an external rulebook but as an internal compass that illuminates God's presence in everyday decisions. The practice of biblical obedience often reveals spiritual insights that remain hidden to casual readers, offering experiential understanding that transcends theoretical knowledge. Through faithful adherence to scriptural wisdom, your spiritual awareness deepens in remarkable ways—truth moves from your head to your heart, abstract concepts become lived realities, and you develop an authentic connection with God that flows naturally from walking in the path He has lovingly prescribed for your highest good.

James 1:22 - "Do not merely listen to the word, and so deceive yourselves. Do what it says."

Obedience to Scripture transforms biblical knowledge from intellectual information into lived reality. This practice acknowledges that God's Word wasn't given merely to inform our thinking but to transform our living—providing not just concepts to consider but commands to follow. True spiritual maturity is measured not by how much Scripture we know but by how faithfully we apply what we know, allowing God's truth to shape our decisions, direct our priorities, and determine our responses to life's challenges.

James' straightforward admonition confronts one of the most common spiritual deceptions—the belief that hearing or understanding God's Word is sufficient without corresponding action. The Greek term for "listen" (akroatēs) referred to someone who attends lectures but never puts the teaching into practice—similar to a person who regularly attends cooking classes but never actually prepares a meal. James insists that such passive reception is not just incomplete but deceptive, creating a false sense of spiritual progress. True engagement with Scripture requires that we move beyond being hearers to becoming doers, allowing God's commands to challenge our natural inclinations and cultural assumptions. This active obedience develops spiritual awareness that recognizes the gap between knowing and doing, prompting us to examine areas where we've embraced God's Word intellectually but resisted it practically. As we consistently practice Scripture-guided living, we experience the truth of Jesus' promise that obedience leads to greater spiritual clarity (John 7:17), creating a virtuous cycle where faithful action leads to deeper understanding, which in turn enables more complete obedience.

16. Rest and Seek the Lord's Presence

Take time to rest in God's presence, allowing His peace to renew your spirit and strengthen your faith. The intentional practice of spiritual rest creates sacred space for divine renewal that can't be found in mere physical relaxation. When you deliberately pause from life's constant activity to simply be in God's presence—without agenda or performance—you're engaging in a profound spiritual discipline that gradually recalibrates your inner awareness. This holy stillness allows divine peace to penetrate layers of anxiety and distraction that often muffle God's gentle voice, creating moments of spiritual clarity that remain elusive in busier seasons. As you consistently prioritize this restful communion, you'll develop heightened sensitivity to God's presence that extends beyond designated prayer times into everyday moments. The practice of spiritual resting teaches your soul to recognize divine peace as its natural state rather than a temporary respite, fundamentally transforming how you process life's challenges. Through faithful seeking of God's presence in quiet moments, your spiritual perception deepens in remarkable ways—subtle divine guidance becomes more recognizable, ordinary experiences reveal extraordinary insights, and you discover the profound truth that authentic spiritual awareness often flourishes not in striving but in the sacred surrender of simply resting in His presence.

Matthew 11:28 - "Come to me, all you who are weary and burdened, and I will give you rest."

Spiritual rest goes beyond physical relaxation to encompass a deep soul-level renewal that can only be found in God's presence. This sacred pause invites us to temporarily set aside our striving, planning, and producing to simply be with God—allowing His peace to permeate our anxieties, His truth to counter our distortions, and His love to heal our wounds. In a culture that often equates worth with productivity, intentional spiritual rest becomes a countercultural declaration that our primary identity isn't rooted in what we accomplish but in whose we are.

Jesus' invitation in Matthew 11:28 speaks directly to those feeling depleted by life's demands—whether from external pressures or self-imposed standards. The Greek word for "rest" (anapauō) suggests not just temporary relief but deep restoration, addressing not merely the symptoms of weariness but its root causes. This divine rest doesn't require elaborate rituals or special locations but simply a willing heart that turns toward Christ in trust. Jesus doesn't demand that we first fix ourselves or become worthy of rest; He simply invites us to come as we are—weary, burdened, and in need. This rest develops spiritual awareness that recognizes our human limitations and embraces our dependence on God, allowing us to release the exhausting illusion of self-sufficiency. As we consistently practice rest in God's presence—whether through Sabbath observance, contemplative prayer, worship, or simply being still before Him—we experience not just renewal of energy but transformation of perspective, returning to our responsibilities with restored clarity, compassion, and purpose.

17. Embrace Silence and Solitude

Set aside moments for silence and solitude to focus on God, listening for His guidance and refreshing your soul. Embracing intentional silence and solitude creates a sacred sanctuary where divine whispers become audible above life's constant noise. When you deliberately step away from distractions to be alone with God—whether for extended retreats or brief daily pauses—you're cultivating spiritual receptivity that allows for deeper communion than typically possible amid constant stimulation. This practice of holy listening gradually refines your spiritual hearing, developing an inner attunement that recognizes God's gentle guidance amid the competing voices clamoring for your attention. As you consistently create these quiet spaces, you'll begin noticing subtle shifts in your spiritual awareness—insights arise unbidden, scripture passages suddenly illuminate with fresh meaning, and you sense divine direction with greater clarity. The discipline of silence teaches your soul the forgotten language of stillness, where God often communicates most profoundly not through dramatic revelation but through the quiet certainty of His presence. Through faithful practice of solitude, your spiritual perception expands beyond intellectual understanding to experiential knowing, cultivating a rich awareness of God's intimate involvement in your life that continues to nourish your soul long after you return to daily responsibilities.

Psalm 46:10 - "Be still, and know that I am God; I will be exalted among the nations, I will be exalted in the earth."

Silence and solitude create sacred space for encountering God without distraction—an intentional stepping away from the noise and demands that typically fill our lives. Unlike isolation, which often stems from fear or avoidance, spiritual solitude is purposeful withdrawal that enables deeper connection with God and clearer discernment of His voice. In these quiet moments, we temporarily silence the external voices competing for our attention and the internal voices of worry, planning, and self-criticism, creating room for God's gentle whisper to be heard.

The command to "be still" in Psalm 46:10 comes in the context of global chaos and upheaval, suggesting that stillness isn't just a luxury for peaceful times but a necessity amid turmoil. The Hebrew phrase "be still" (raphah) literally means to let drop or let go—conveying the release of striving, controlling, and anxious activity. This stillness leads to knowing God, not merely intellectually but experientially, recognizing His sovereignty even when circumstances suggest otherwise. The resulting awareness of God's exaltation—both present and future—provides perspective that transcends immediate struggles. When we practice silence and solitude, we develop spiritual sensitivity that can distinguish God's voice from competing influences, recognize His movements in subtle promptings, and align our hearts with His purposes. These quiet spaces often become moments of profound transformation where God reshapes our priorities, heals our hurts, and reveals aspects of His character that might go unnoticed in our usual busyness. Far from being unproductive time, these moments of stillness become the foundation for more authentic living and effective service.

18. Cultivate Empathy to the Lord and Others

Develop a deep understanding and sensitivity to the feelings and spiritual needs of others, as well as a heartfelt connection with God. The practice of spiritual empathy creates a profound dual connection that transforms both your relationship with God and your interactions with others. When you deliberately cultivate sensitivity to the divine heart—seeking to understand what moves God and attuning yourself to His perspectives—you develop spiritual perception that recognizes holy invitations in everyday moments. This same empathetic awareness, when extended to others, allows you to perceive spiritual needs beneath surface behaviors, discerning hurts and hopes that might otherwise remain hidden. As this practice deepens, you'll notice your prayers shifting from monologue to dialogue as you become more attuned to God's responses, while your human relationships develop a sacred dimension that sees beyond external appearances to the divine image within each person. This empathetic posture gradually reshapes your spiritual awareness, helping you recognize God's presence in unexpected places—in the vulnerable sharing of a struggling friend, in the wordless communion of compassionate presence, or in moments when your heart breaks for what breaks His. Through consistent cultivation of holy empathy, you develop a richly textured spiritual sensitivity that experiences God not just in formal religious settings but in the beautiful, complex landscape of human connection.

Philippians 2:4 - "Let each of you look not only to his own interests, but also to the interests of others."

Empathy creates bridges of understanding that connect us more authentically both with God and with those around us. This spiritual capacity enables us to move beyond surface-level interactions to genuine connection—sensing others' unspoken needs, recognizing the emotions behind their words, and responding with appropriate compassion. Divine empathy extends this sensitivity to our relationship with God, helping us attune to His heart for humanity and discern His movements in our lives and communities.

Paul's exhortation in Philippians challenges our natural self-focus, calling us to intentionally shift our attention to others' concerns and needs. The Greek term for "look" (skopeō) suggests careful observation and deliberate focus—not just casual awareness but attentive consideration. This empathetic vision requires both spiritual insight and intentional practice, training ourselves to ask not just "What do I need?" but "What might others be experiencing?" and "What would honor God in this situation?" As we cultivate this outward-focused perspective, we develop spiritual awareness that recognizes the divine image in every person we encounter, seeing beyond behavior to the underlying needs, hopes, and hurts. This empathetic understanding transforms our interactions—whether listening to a friend's struggles without rushing to solutions, celebrating another's success without comparison, or engaging thoughtfully with viewpoints different from our own. Through consistent practice of empathy, we participate in Christ's incarnational ministry, entering others' worlds as He entered ours, and making His compassionate presence tangible through our attentive care.

19. Use Work and Creativity to Resonate

Utilize your work and creative endeavors as expressions of your faith, making them resonate with God's purpose for your life. Infusing your work and creative pursuits with spiritual intention transforms ordinary tasks into sacred offerings that resonate with divine purpose. When you deliberately approach your vocation and creative expressions as extensions of your faith—whether through artistic endeavors, professional responsibilities, or daily tasks—you create a powerful integration that dissolves the artificial boundary between "spiritual life" and "everyday life." This mindful practice gradually refines your spiritual awareness, helping you recognize divine inspiration in moments of creative flow and God's guiding hand in professional opportunities or challenges. As this integrated perspective deepens, you'll begin experiencing your work not merely as obligation but as collaboration with the Creator, discovering profound spiritual insights that emerge uniquely through your particular skills and contributions. The practice of spiritually resonant work cultivates a heightened sensitivity to God's presence in seemingly secular spaces, allowing you to perceive divine purpose in tasks others might consider mundane. Through faithful stewardship of your creative gifts and vocational calling, your spiritual perception expands beyond traditional religious contexts into a rich awareness of how God is working through your unique contributions to bring beauty, order, and restoration to the world around you.

Colossians 3:23-24 - "Whatever you do, work heartily, as for the Lord and not for men, knowing that from the Lord you will receive the inheritance as your reward. You are serving the Lord Christ."

Work and creativity take on profound spiritual significance when we recognize them as divine callings rather than merely secular activities. This perspective transforms our approach to daily tasks—whether building a spreadsheet, caring for children, designing a solution, or creating art—elevating them from obligations to opportunities for worship. When our work resonates with God's purposes, we participate in His ongoing creative activity in the world, using our unique gifts and positions to bring order, beauty, justice, and flourishing to the spaces we influence.

Paul's instruction to the Colossian believers—many of whom were slaves with little control over their work—reveals that the spiritual value of our labor doesn't depend on its visibility, status, or compensation but on the heart and purpose behind it. The phrase "work heartily" translates a Greek expression that literally means "from the soul"—suggesting wholehearted engagement rather than halfhearted compliance. This God-centered motivation transforms even mundane tasks by redirecting our ultimate audience from human approval to divine recognition. When we internalize the reality that "you are serving the Lord Christ" in every dimension of our work, we develop spiritual awareness that discerns opportunities for excellence, integrity, and witness in our daily responsibilities. This resonant approach to work creates a powerful integration between faith and vocation, eliminating the artificial divide between "sacred" and "secular" activities and allowing our entire life to become an arena for spiritual formation and kingdom influence.

20. Sing, Laugh, Smile, and Choose Happiness

Embrace joy in your life through singing, laughter, and smiles, choosing happiness that reflects the joy of your faith. The practice of faith-filled joy creates a powerful spiritual current that transforms both your inner landscape and your witness to the world. When you deliberately choose to express happiness through singing, genuine laughter, and warm smiles—even during challenging seasons—you're engaging in a profound spiritual discipline that aligns your emotional experience with the deeper joy that transcends circumstances. This joyful posture gradually reshapes your spiritual awareness, helping you recognize divine goodness in moments that might otherwise seem ordinary or difficult. As this practice deepens, you'll notice a subtle shift in your perception—worship becomes less about dutiful observance and more about authentic celebration, while your capacity to experience God's presence expands beyond solemn moments into expressions of holy delight. The habit of choosing joy serves as a tangible reminder of the freedom found in faith, cultivating a contagious spiritual vitality that often speaks more eloquently of God's goodness than formal testimony. Through consistent cultivation of these joyful expressions, your spiritual sensitivity develops a richer texture that perceives divine presence not just in reverent silence but in the sacred echoes of laughter and song that reflect the abundant life Christ promised to those who follow Him.

Psalm 100:2 - "Serve the Lord with gladness; come before him with joyful songs."

Joy represents one of the most compelling witnesses to our faith—a quality that distinguishes believers not by their freedom from troubles but by their transcendent response to life's challenges. Biblical joy isn't dependent on favorable circumstances but is rooted in the unchanging character of God and the unshakable reality of His promises. When we sing, laugh, and smile as expressions of this deeper joy, we declare our confidence in a good God who remains worthy of praise even in difficult seasons.

The psalmist's invitation to "serve the Lord with gladness" challenges the solemn, duty-bound approach to spirituality that can characterize religious observance. The Hebrew term for "gladness" (simchah) conveys vibrant delight and celebration, suggesting that our service to God should be characterized by genuine pleasure rather than grim obligation. This instruction to approach God with "joyful songs" recognizes the unique capacity of music and vocal expression to bypass our intellectual defenses and touch our deepest emotions. When we intentionally cultivate expressions of joy—whether through worship music, appreciation of beauty, celebration of blessings, or simply choosing to smile—we develop spiritual awareness that recognizes God's goodness even amid challenges. This joy-filled orientation doesn't deny suffering or minimize grief but rather places them within the larger context of God's faithful presence and ultimate redemption. As we practice choosing happiness rooted in divine reality rather than fleeting circumstances, we offer a compelling alternative to both shallow optimism and cynical pessimism, demonstrating the authentic, resilient joy that characterizes kingdom living.

21. Foster a Godly Sense of Awe and Wonder

Nurture a deep sense of reverence and admiration for God's creation and His works, which inspires humility and gratitude. The mindful development of sacred awe creates a transformative spiritual lens that reveals divine majesty in both spectacular vistas and ordinary moments. When you deliberately pause to marvel at creation's intricate design—from sweeping starlit skies to the precise patterns of a single snowflake—you're engaging in a profound spiritual practice that recalibrates your perception of both God and self. This wonder-filled perspective gradually deepens your spiritual awareness, helping you recognize divine fingerprints in experiences that might otherwise seem commonplace. As this practice of holy amazement becomes more ingrained, you'll notice a beautiful paradox emerging—the more you comprehend God's vastness, the more intimately you sense His presence in personal ways. The habit of standing in reverent wonder serves as a natural antidote to spiritual pride and entitlement, fostering a humble gratitude that recognizes even breath itself as unmerited gift. Through consistent attentiveness to awe-inspiring moments, your spiritual sensitivity expands beyond intellectual understanding to experiential worship, cultivating a rich awareness of God's immanence and transcendence that transforms routine experiences into encounters with the divine presence that permeates all of creation.

Psalm 33:8 - "Let all the earth fear the Lord; let all the inhabitants of the world stand in awe of Him."

Awe and wonder awaken our spiritual senses to the majesty of God, breaking through the numbness of familiarity that can diminish our appreciation of both creation and Creator. This sacred amazement—whether triggered by a star-filled sky, a newborn's tiny fingers, the intricacies of a cell, or the story of redemption—reminds us that we live in a world saturated with divine fingerprints. When we cultivate this posture of wonder, ordinary moments become opportunities for worship as we recognize glimpses of God's character reflected throughout His handiwork.

The psalmist's call for universal awe employs the Hebrew term for "fear" (yare), which encompasses not just reverence but astonished admiration—a response that acknowledges both God's transcendent greatness and our comparative smallness. This holy awe differs from mere aesthetic appreciation by recognizing the Creator behind the creation, moving beyond "isn't this beautiful?" to "what does this reveal about the One who made it?" When we intentionally nurture this sense of wonder—whether by studying the cosmos, exploring nature, contemplating Scripture's depths, or simply pausing to really see what we typically overlook—we develop spiritual awareness that perceives divine presence in previously unnoticed places. This wonder-filled perspective protects us from both casual familiarity with God and cold intellectualism about Him, keeping our spiritual journey fresh and vibrant. As we consistently practice awe-inspired observation, even familiar Scripture passages, church practices, and daily routines become opportunities for renewed appreciation of God's wisdom, power, and loving attention to detail.

22. Live Meaningfully with Eternal Perspective

Align your daily life and decisions with the eternal truths of God's Word, focusing on what lasts beyond the temporal. Cultivating an eternal perspective fundamentally transforms how you navigate daily choices by anchoring them to divine significance rather than fleeting cultural values. When you deliberately filter decisions through the lens of eternity—considering their spiritual impact beyond immediate gratification—you develop a deeper awareness that distinguishes between what merely satisfies momentary desires and what truly matters in God's economy. This eternal mindset gradually refines your spiritual discernment, helping you recognize divine invitations in ordinary moments and invest your limited time and resources in pursuits with lasting significance. As this perspective becomes more integrated into your thinking, you'll experience a profound spiritual freedom from the tyranny of urgency and comparison that often clouds spiritual vision. The practice of living with eternity in view creates a meaningful framework that connects your present actions with God's ongoing redemptive narrative, fostering a richer spiritual awareness that perceives divine purpose threading through even the most routine aspects of your daily journey.

Colossians 3:2 - "Set your minds on things above, not on earthly things."

An eternal perspective transforms how we evaluate everything—from daily choices to major life decisions—by measuring them against the backdrop of eternity rather than temporary impact. This heavenly mindset doesn't dismiss earthly responsibilities but rather infuses them with transcendent purpose, helping us distinguish between what is merely urgent and what is truly important. When we align our priorities with eternal values, we invest our limited time, energy, and resources in pursuits that will matter not just tomorrow or next year, but in the light of eternity.

Paul's instruction to the Colossians presents this mindset shift as an intentional reorientation—actively setting our thoughts on "things above." The Greek term for "set your minds" (phroneō) involves more than casual thinking; it suggests deep consideration that shapes our values, desires, and actions. This heavenly focus doesn't promote impractical otherworldliness but rather brings clarity to our earthly engagement, helping us recognize which aspects of our daily lives have eternal significance. As we practice this eternal-minded living, we develop spiritual awareness that discerns which investments yield lasting returns—relationships nurtured, character developed, faith shared, and service rendered—versus those that offer only temporary satisfaction. This perspective liberates us from both the tyranny of urgent trivialities and the despair of present difficulties, placing all of life within the larger story of God's redemptive purposes. Each decision becomes an opportunity to align with what ultimately matters, creating a life of profound meaning that resonates beyond our limited years into God's eternal kingdom.

23. Prioritize Integrity, Values, and Beliefs

Uphold strong moral principles and biblical values in all aspects of life, demonstrating integrity in your actions. Anchoring your life in unwavering integrity creates a powerful spiritual foundation that illuminates God's presence in everyday decisions. When you consistently align your actions with biblical values—especially when doing so comes at personal cost—you're engaging in a profound spiritual practice that transcends religious performance. This commitment to moral coherence gradually refines your spiritual discernment, developing an inner clarity that recognizes divine guidance with increasing confidence amid complex ethical landscapes. As this principled living becomes more habitual, you'll notice your spiritual awareness deepening in remarkable ways—your conscience becomes more finely tuned to God's voice, your witness gains authentic credibility, and you experience the profound freedom that comes from internal alignment rather than compartmentalized faith. The practice of integrity-centered living creates a transparent vessel through which God's character becomes visible to others, cultivating a rich spiritual sensitivity that experiences His pleasure not just in religious moments but in the sacred territory of everyday ethical choices.

Proverbs 10:9 - "Whoever walks in integrity walks securely, but whoever takes crooked paths will be found out."

Integrity unifies our public and private selves into a consistent whole, aligning our actions with our professed beliefs regardless of who is watching. This moral wholeness represents more than just avoiding deception—it actively pursues truthfulness, reliability, and ethical consistency in every dimension of life. When we prioritize integrity, we refuse to compartmentalize our faith, recognizing that God's standards apply equally to our business dealings, online activity, family relationships, and personal habits.

Solomon's wisdom highlights the practical benefit of integrity: security. The Hebrew word for "integrity" (tom) conveys completeness and soundness—a life without moral fractures or ethical inconsistencies. This wholeness creates stability that transcends circumstances, allowing us to walk confidently without fear of exposure or contradictions being discovered. The contrasting image of "crooked paths" suggests deception that may temporarily appear advantageous but ultimately leads to exposure and instability. When we consistently practice integrity—keeping our promises, speaking truthfully, honoring commitments, and making ethical choices even when costly—we develop spiritual awareness that recognizes temptations toward compromise more quickly and responds with principled resistance. This integrity-centered approach to life becomes increasingly countercultural in a world that often celebrates expediency over principle and results over process. Yet as we maintain alignment between our beliefs and behaviors, we offer a compelling witness to the transformative power of faith, demonstrating that kingdom values create not just moral distinctiveness but genuine freedom and security.

24. Choose to be Christlike in All Ways

Strive to embody the character and teachings of Jesus Christ in your behavior, relationships, and life choices. Intentionally modeling your life after Christ's example creates a transformative spiritual framework that reshapes your entire approach to existence. When you deliberately filter your responses, decisions, and attitudes through the lens of Jesus's character—choosing patience when provoked, compassion over judgment, or service instead of self-promotion—you're engaging in profound spiritual formation that goes beyond religious obligation. This Christlike orientation gradually refines your spiritual awareness, developing an inner sensitivity that recognizes divine invitations to embody specific aspects of Jesus's nature in everyday encounters. As this practice deepens, you'll begin experiencing scripture not as abstract teaching but as lived reality, finding that your capacity to perceive God's presence expands as your character increasingly reflects His Son's. The commitment to Christlikeness creates a beautiful spiritual coherence where your inner convictions and outer actions harmonize, cultivating a rich awareness of God's transforming work in your life that others can recognize through the authentic reflection of Jesus they encounter in your words and deeds.

Ephesians 5:1-2 - "Follow God's example, therefore, as dearly loved children and walk in the way of love, just as Christ loved us and gave himself up for us as a fragrant offering and sacrifice to God."

Christlikeness represents the ultimate goal of spiritual formation—the gradual transformation of our character, priorities, and responses to increasingly reflect those of Jesus. This deliberate imitation goes beyond external behaviors to encompass inner attitudes, motivations, and values that shaped Christ's life and ministry. When we choose to be Christlike, we embrace His compassion for the marginalized, His courage in confronting injustice, His humility in serving others, His obedience to the Father's will, and His sacrificial love that puts others' needs before personal comfort.

Paul's exhortation frames this imitation not as burdensome obligation but as the natural response of "dearly loved children" who model themselves after their Father. The primary characteristic we're called to emulate is love—not merely affectionate feeling but sacrificial action that seeks others' highest good regardless of personal cost. The reference to Christ's self-giving as a "fragrant offering" suggests that our Christlike choices create a spiritual aroma that pleases God and influences those around us. As we practice Christlike responses in daily situations—choosing patience when provoked, extending grace when wronged, speaking truth with kindness, serving without recognition—we develop spiritual awareness that increasingly recognizes "What would Jesus do?" not as a cliché but as a transformative filter for our decisions. This ongoing conformity to Christ's image doesn't happen instantly but progressively, as consistent small choices accumulate into significant character development. Through this intentional pursuit of Christlikeness, we fulfill our created purpose, reflecting God's nature to a world desperately in need of encountering His love in tangible form.

25. Love God, Yourself, and Others

Embrace the greatest commandments by loving God with all your heart, treating yourself with kindness, and extending love to others. Practicing threefold love creates a profound spiritual ecosystem where divine presence flows naturally through every relationship. When you deliberately prioritize loving God wholeheartedly, extending compassion to yourself, and genuinely caring for others, you're engaging with the very essence of Christ's teaching rather than merely following religious rules. This integrated love approach gradually transforms your spiritual awareness, helping you recognize God's presence not just in formal worship but in moments of self-compassion and human connection that might otherwise seem ordinary. As this practice deepens, you'll notice your spiritual perception expanding beyond compartmentalized faith to a holistic experience where loving God naturally overflows into how you treat yourself and others. The commitment to this love-centered spirituality creates a beautiful alignment with divine design, cultivating a rich spiritual sensitivity that experiences God's presence most tangibly when you're fully engaged in the sacred practice of giving and receiving love in all its dimensions.

Matthew 22:37-39 - "Jesus replied: 'Love the Lord your God with all your heart and with all your soul and with all your mind.' This is the first and greatest commandment. And the second is like it: 'Love your neighbor as yourself.'"

Love stands as the central, defining characteristic of authentic spirituality—not as one virtue among many but as the foundational principle that encompasses and energizes all others. This three-dimensional love creates a comprehensive framework for spiritual awareness: upward love toward God, inward love toward self, and outward love toward others. When these dimensions exist in proper balance, they create a spiritually and emotionally healthy life that reflects God's character and fulfills our created purpose.

Jesus' response to the question about the greatest commandment reveals that love isn't merely one aspect of spiritual maturity but its very essence. His instruction to love God "with all your heart, soul, and mind" calls for comprehensive devotion that engages every dimension of our being—our emotions, will, thoughts, and actions all oriented toward God as our supreme treasure. The second commandment builds upon this foundation, directing us to extend to others the same care, respect, and concern we naturally afford ourselves. This commandment implicitly acknowledges the importance of appropriate self-love, not as self-absorption but as recognition of our worth as image-bearers whom God values. As we practice this balanced love—prioritizing devotion to God, treating ourselves with grace-filled kindness, and extending compassionate care to others—we develop spiritual awareness that recognizes opportunities to express love in concrete ways. From this love-centered foundation, all other spiritual practices find their proper motivation and expression, protecting us from both legalistic rule-following and self-serving spirituality. Each loving choice, whether toward God, self, or others, becomes a participation in the very nature of God, who is Himself love (1 John 4:8).

Self-Awareness: The Next 25 Ways

Self-awareness is the conscious knowledge of one's own character, feelings, motives, and desires—a reflective capacity that allows us to understand not just what we do but why we do it. From a biblical perspective, this introspective understanding isn't merely psychological self-analysis but spiritual discernment that recognizes how our thoughts, emotions, and behaviors align with or diverge from God's design. It's about developing an honest understanding of both our God-given strengths and our fallen tendencies, allowing the Holy Spirit to illuminate areas where transformation is needed.

Many believers struggle with persistent patterns of behavior they cannot seem to change, often because they lack awareness of the underlying beliefs, fears, or wounds driving these actions. Others find themselves repeatedly surprised by their emotional reactions, experiencing feelings that seem disproportionate or disconnected from present circumstances. The dissonance between our outward Christian identity and our internal reality can create shame and isolation, making us reluctant to acknowledge our struggles even to ourselves. Without self-awareness, we may unknowingly project our unresolved issues onto others, damaging relationships and hindering our spiritual growth.

Developing true self-awareness brings profound freedom as we move from being controlled by unconscious patterns to making conscious, Spirit-led choices. There's deep satisfaction in understanding the design behind our unique personality, recognizing our spiritual gifts, and deploying our strengths in service to God's purposes. Self-awareness creates the possibility for authentic community as we bring our true selves—not just our curated image—into relationship with God and others. This honesty before God opens the door to experiencing His grace more deeply, as we find Him accepting and transforming the very parts of ourselves we've been afraid to acknowledge.

Self-awareness develops gradually through simple but consistent practices that can be integrated into daily life. Beginning with regular moments of reflection—perhaps at the day's end—helps us notice patterns in our reactions and interactions. Learning to ask yourself thoughtful questions (What am I feeling right now? Why might I be responding this way?) develops the habit of healthy introspection. Feedback from trusted friends and mentors provides valuable external perspective that complements our internal observations. Scripture reading becomes more transformative when approached not just for information but for self-revelation, allowing God's Word to "judge the thoughts and attitudes of the heart" (Hebrews 4:12).

Scripture consistently affirms the importance of accurate self-knowledge, from David's prayer "Search me, O God, and know my heart... See if there is any offensive way in me" (Psalm 139:23-24) to Paul's exhortation that "everyone should examine themselves" (1 Corinthians 11:28). Jesus himself emphasized that transformation begins within, addressing the heart's condition rather than merely modifying external behaviors (Matthew 23:25-26). The biblical portrayal of spiritual formation always involves growing self-awareness as we "take off the old self" and "put on the new self" (Ephesians 4:22-24), a process that requires honest recognition of both what needs to be discarded and what needs to be developed.

At the EIQ2 EI Learning Center, we recognize that emotional intelligence begins with self-awareness—the foundation upon which all other emotional competencies are built. The following 25 ways to deepen your self-awareness incorporate principles that bridge psychological insights with biblical wisdom, offering practical steps toward understanding yourself as God created you to be. Each concept builds upon the understanding that truly knowing yourself is inseparable from knowing God, for it is in His light that "we see light" (Psalm 36:9)—including the light of accurate self-perception.

26. Affirm Who God Says You Are

Recognize and affirm your identity and worth as defined by God, not by worldly standards or opinions. Embracing your God-defined identity creates a powerful spiritual anchor that transforms how you view yourself and navigate life's challenges. When you intentionally see yourself through God's eyes instead of cultural expectations or others' opinions, you establish an unshakable foundation that remains steady regardless of circumstances. This practice deepens your spiritual awareness by helping you distinguish between God's affirming voice and the critical thoughts that distort self-perception. As you consistently align your self-understanding with biblical truths, you'll develop clearer recognition of when negative self-talk contradicts divine perspective. This habit of affirming your God-given worth reveals where worldly values have influenced your thinking, cultivating a richer self-awareness that distinguishes between temporary validation and eternal value. Through this practice, your spiritual perception expands beyond external judgments to a profound understanding of your true identity in God, transforming both your self-concept and how you relate to others from a place of genuine security rather than approval-seeking.

1 Peter 2:9 - "But you are a chosen people, a royal priesthood, a holy nation, God's special possession, that you may declare the praises of him who called you out of darkness into his wonderful light."

Identity forms the foundation of how we see ourselves, relate to others, and approach life's challenges. When we derive our primary identity from God's declarations rather than from shifting cultural values, others' opinions, or even our own accomplishments, we establish an unshakable core of self-understanding. This divine identity isn't based on performance or comparison but on God's sovereign choice and gracious love, providing stability that transcends circumstance and external validation.

Peter's powerful declaration addresses believers who lived as minorities in a hostile culture, reminding them that their true significance came not from social status but from spiritual reality. The language he uses—"chosen people," "royal priesthood," "holy nation," "God's special possession"—intentionally applies to the church terms originally used for Israel, emphasizing the profound dignity and purpose God bestows on His people. This identity carries both privilege and responsibility, as indicated by the purpose clause: "that you may declare the praises..." When we internalize these divine affirmations, we develop self-awareness that recognizes the disconnect between how God sees us and how the world might define us. This awareness allows us to navigate criticism without devastation, success without arrogance, and failure without identity crisis. As we consistently affirm who God says we are—through Scripture meditation, truth-based declarations, and community reinforcement—we experience growing freedom from unhealthy approval-seeking, performance-based worth, and fear-driven choices. Our self-perception gradually aligns with divine reality, enabling us to live from a place of secure belonging rather than anxious striving.

27. Choose to Act 'As unto the Lord'

Dedicate every action and decision to God, performing each task with dedication as if directly serving Him. Approaching each task as an offering to God transforms ordinary responsibilities into sacred opportunities for spiritual connection. When you intentionally dedicate your work, relationships, and daily choices to God—treating even mundane activities as acts of worship—you create a powerful spiritual mindfulness that infuses everyday moments with divine purpose. This practice gradually refines your awareness of God's presence in all aspects of life, helping you recognize that the artificial divide between "spiritual" and "secular" activities dissolves when everything is done as service to Him. As this perspective becomes more ingrained, you'll notice a shift in both your motivation and perception—tasks once viewed as burdensome become meaningful expressions of devotion, while your capacity to experience God expands beyond formal religious settings into the workshop, kitchen, office, or classroom. The habit of working "as unto the Lord" creates a beautiful integrity to your spiritual life, cultivating a deeper self-awareness that perceives divine invitation and purpose in even the most routine responsibilities, ultimately transforming not just how you perform tasks but how you experience God's presence throughout your daily journey.

Colossians 3:23 - "Whatever you do, work at it with all your heart, as working for the Lord, not for human masters."

Acting "as unto the Lord" transforms ordinary activities into sacred offerings by redirecting our focus from human approval to divine purpose. This mindset shift elevates seemingly mundane tasks—whether completing paperwork, cleaning a home, serving a customer, or attending a meeting—into opportunities for worship and witness. When we approach our responsibilities with this God-centered motivation, the quality of our work becomes a reflection of our reverence for Him rather than merely a response to external expectations or rewards.

Paul's instruction to the Colossians addresses the challenging context of slavery, showing that even in the most oppressive circumstances, believers could find dignity and purpose by recognizing Christ as their ultimate audience. The phrase "with all your heart" translates a Greek expression that literally means "from the soul," suggesting wholehearted engagement rather than mere compliance. This divine perspective transforms our motivation, effort, and attitude—whether anyone else notices or appreciates our diligence. As we practice this God-conscious approach to daily tasks, we develop self-awareness that recognizes when we're slipping into performance driven by human approval or resentment due to lack of recognition. This awareness allows us to realign our motivation, reclaiming the joy and purpose that come from serving Christ in everything. Each conscious choice to work "as unto the Lord" strengthens our spiritual muscles, gradually forming habits of excellence and integrity that manifest regardless of who is watching. This consistent, quality-driven approach to life's responsibilities becomes a powerful, often wordless testimony to the difference Christ makes in the life of a believer.

28. Be at Peace with God, Yourself, and Others

Cultivate a life of peace by reconciling with God, forgiving yourself, and maintaining harmonious relationships with others. The intentional practice of holistic peace creates a powerful spiritual ecosystem where your relationship with God naturally influences how you view yourself and interact with others. When you prioritize reconciliation in these three vital connections—restoring fellowship with God, practicing self-compassion, and pursuing harmony in relationships—you establish a foundation for authentic spiritual growth that transcends religious performance. This integrated approach helps you develop greater self-awareness, enabling you to recognize when something is disrupting your inner tranquility and trace it to its source, whether divine, personal, or interpersonal. As you cultivate consistent peace in these areas, you'll notice increased sensitivity to spiritual dissonance—moments when unforgiveness, self-criticism, or relational conflict are hindering your spiritual wellness. The practice of maintaining this threefold harmony creates a transparent spiritual clarity where unresolved issues become more readily apparent, fostering deeper self-understanding and a more genuine experience of God's presence as peace becomes not just an emotional state but a spiritual orientation that influences every dimension of your life.

Romans 12:18 - "If it is possible, as far as it depends on you, live at peace with everyone."

Peace exists in three vital dimensions—with God, within ourselves, and with others—forming a comprehensive tranquility that stabilizes our entire being. This multi-faceted peace begins with reconciliation with God through Christ, which establishes the foundation for inner harmony and healthy relationships. When we experience peace in all three dimensions, we demonstrate the integrating power of the gospel, which restores the relationships fractured by sin and creates wholeness where division once reigned.

Paul's instruction acknowledges both the importance and the challenge of peaceful relationships, recognizing that reconciliation requires mutual participation. The qualifying phrases—"if it is possible" and "as far as it depends on you"—reveal a realistic understanding that peace isn't always achievable despite our best efforts. Some conflicts remain unresolved due to others' choices, which we cannot control. Nevertheless, this command places clear responsibility on believers to take initiative in pursuing peace—removing obstacles, seeking understanding, offering forgiveness, and demonstrating patience. As we practice this peace-making approach to relationships, we develop self-awareness that recognizes our own contributions to conflict, our triggers for defensive reactions, and our capacity for reconciliation. This awareness allows us to respond thoughtfully rather than react impulsively when tensions arise, creating space for the Holy Spirit to work in challenging situations. The consistent pursuit of peace—while never compromising truth or righteousness—becomes a distinctive mark of Christ's followers in a world characterized by division, demonstrating the transformative reality of the "peace that passes understanding" (Philippians 4:7).

29. Exercise Self-Care

Take care of your physical, mental, and spiritual well-being to serve God and others effectively. The practice of intentional self-care establishes a vital foundation for authentic spiritual vitality that honors God's design for wholeness. When you deliberately attend to your physical needs, mental health, and spiritual nourishment as interconnected aspects of your being—rather than compartmentalizing them—you're recognizing that stewardship of yourself is a sacred responsibility rather than selfish indulgence. This holistic approach gradually deepens your self-awareness, helping you recognize when depletion in one area is affecting your overall spiritual wellness and capacity to fulfill your calling. As you consistently prioritize balanced self-care, you'll develop heightened sensitivity to the subtle signals your body, mind, and spirit provide before burnout occurs, allowing you to respond with wisdom rather than pushing beyond healthy limits. The habit of caring for yourself creates a sustainable framework for service, cultivating richer spiritual awareness of how your physical and emotional state influences your ability to perceive God's presence and extend His love to others. Through faithful stewardship of your whole self, you honor the temple God has entrusted to you while developing deeper understanding of your unique needs and limitations—essential knowledge for authentic spiritual growth and effective ministry.

1 Corinthians 6:19-20 - "Do you not know that your bodies are temples of the Holy Spirit, who is in you, whom you have received from God? You are not your own; you were bought at a price. Therefore honor God with your bodies."

Self-care from a biblical perspective differs fundamentally from self-indulgence—it's not about pampering or entitlement but about responsible stewardship of the resources God has entrusted to us. This holistic care encompasses our physical health through appropriate rest, nutrition, and exercise; our mental well-being through thought management and emotional processing; and our spiritual vitality through consistent spiritual disciplines. When we practice biblical self-care, we acknowledge that our energy, health, and capacity are finite resources to be managed wisely rather than exploited recklessly.

Paul's powerful metaphor of our bodies as "temples of the Holy Spirit" elevates physical stewardship from a personal preference to a spiritual responsibility. Just as the Jerusalem temple was maintained with reverence and care as God's dwelling place, our bodies deserve thoughtful attention as vessels containing God's presence. The reminder that we were "bought at a price" places self-care within the context of redemption—we maintain our well-being not primarily for our own benefit but to honor the One who purchased us through Christ's sacrifice. As we practice intentional self-care—whether by establishing healthy boundaries, scheduling necessary rest, nourishing our bodies properly, or processing emotions honestly—we develop self-awareness that recognizes our limitations and needs without shame. This awareness allows us to acknowledge when we're approaching burnout, requiring renewal, or developing unhealthy patterns, enabling timely course corrections before damage occurs. Through consistent, holistic self-care, we position ourselves for sustainable service and witness, demonstrating that honoring God includes honoring His design for human flourishing.

30. Be Self-Confident and Have Self-Worth

Embrace the confidence and value that come from being a child of God, knowing He has created you with purpose and love. God-centered confidence creates a transformative spiritual foundation that fundamentally reorients your self-perception. When you deliberately ground your sense of worth in your identity as God's beloved creation—rather than in fleeting accomplishments or others' approval—you establish an unshakable core that remains steady amid life's inevitable fluctuations. This divinely-anchored self-worth gradually deepens your self-awareness, helping you distinguish between healthy confidence that acknowledges your God-given value and prideful self-reliance that dismisses your need for Him. As you consistently affirm your worth as defined by your Creator, you'll develop heightened sensitivity to how cultural messages about success and value often contradict biblical truth, allowing you to recognize and reject false metrics of worthiness. The habit of seeing yourself through God's eyes illuminates areas where insecurity has limited your spiritual growth or service, cultivating a richer awareness of both your inherent dignity and your complete dependence on Him. Through this balanced practice of spiritual confidence, your perception expands beyond worldly standards to a profound understanding of your true worth—not earned through performance but eternally secured through God's unfailing love and purposeful design.

Ephesians 2:10 - "For we are God's handiwork, created in Christ Jesus to do good works, which God prepared in advance for us to do."

Godly self-confidence differs profoundly from prideful self-reliance—it's not arrogance about our own abilities but humble assurance in our God-given identity and purpose. This confidence rests not on comparing ourselves favorably to others or achieving impressive accomplishments, but on the unshakable foundation of being intentionally created, unconditionally loved, and specifically designed by God. When we cultivate this faith-based confidence, we can pursue our calling without being paralyzed by fear of failure or others' opinions, recognizing that our ultimate worth is established by God's view of us rather than human assessment.

Paul's beautiful description of believers as God's "handiwork" employs the Greek term poiēma (from which we get our word "poem"), suggesting that we are divine artistic expressions—carefully crafted rather than mass-produced. This creative intentionality extends to the purpose for which we were made: "good works" that God has "prepared in advance" specifically for us to accomplish. This revelation infuses our identity with tremendous significance, assuring us that we have essential contributions to make that align with how we've been uniquely designed. As we embrace this truth, we develop self-awareness that distinguishes between false humility (which denies our gifts and value) and genuine humility (which acknowledges both our God-given strengths and our complete dependence on Him). This awareness allows us to step into opportunities with appropriate confidence, offering our abilities without either self-deprecation or self-importance. Through consistently viewing ourselves through God's perspective, we establish a stable sense of worth that isn't vulnerable to the shifting sands of performance, appearance, or others' approval.

31. Accept Responsible Vulnerability

Be open about your weaknesses and struggles, trusting in God's strength and the support of the faithful community. When you deliberately acknowledge your weaknesses and struggles—sharing them appropriately with God and trusted others—you're embracing a profound spiritual discipline that reflects authentic faith rather than spiritual pretense. This courageous openness gradually deepens your self-awareness, helping you recognize areas where pride or fear have hindered genuine spiritual growth and honest relationship with God and others. As you consistently practice appropriate vulnerability, you'll develop heightened sensitivity to the difference between healthy transparency that invites growth and unfiltered disclosure that lacks wisdom or boundaries. The habit of acknowledging your limitations creates space for experiencing God's strength in tangible ways, cultivating richer spiritual awareness of how divine power manifests most visibly in your areas of acknowledged weakness. Through faithful practice of responsible vulnerability, your spiritual perception expands beyond self-reliance to a profound experience of community and grace, ultimately transforming how you understand both your limitations and God's sufficiency in the midst of your human frailty.

2 Corinthians 12:9 - "But he said to me, 'My grace is sufficient for you, for my power is made perfect in weakness.' Therefore I will boast all the more gladly about my weaknesses, so that Christ's power may rest on me."

Responsible vulnerability creates authentic connection by allowing others to see our true selves rather than carefully curated images. This openness differs from indiscriminate transparency or emotional dumping—it involves discerning what to share, with whom, and when, always with the purpose of fostering growth and glorifying God. When we practice this balanced vulnerability, we create spaces where others feel safe to be genuine, breaking the isolation that comes from pretending to have everything together and enabling the body of Christ to function as it was designed—with members bearing one another's burdens.

Paul's profound testimony reveals a counterintuitive spiritual principle: acknowledging weakness becomes the pathway to experiencing God's strength. After pleading for relief from his "thorn in the flesh," Paul received not healing but a transformative perspective—that his limitation created space for divine power to be displayed. His response challenges our natural tendency to hide, minimize, or apologize for our weaknesses, inviting us instead to "boast" about them as opportunities for Christ's power to be manifested. As we practice this vulnerable authenticity—whether by confessing struggles, asking for help, sharing disappointments, or admitting limitations—we develop self-awareness that recognizes our tendency toward both protective self-sufficiency and unhealthy self-exposure. This awareness allows us to navigate vulnerability with wisdom, knowing when disclosure serves redemptive purposes versus when it might burden others unnecessarily. Through consistent practice of responsible vulnerability, we create communities characterized by genuine connection rather than superficial impression management, where God's grace becomes tangibly evident in our mutual support and collective dependence on His strength.

32. Become Transformed through God's Grace

Allow God's grace to change you from the inside out, leading to a life that reflects His love and truth. Surrendering to grace-driven transformation creates a profound spiritual foundation that transcends mere behavioral modification. When you deliberately open yourself to God's transformative work—allowing divine love to reshape your character from within rather than simply conforming to external religious expectations—you're engaging with the heart of authentic spiritual growth. Through faithful surrender to this transformative process, your spiritual perception expands beyond self-improvement to a profound experience of God's patient, persistent work within you, fundamentally changing how you understand both your struggles and your growth as evidence of grace actively reshaping you into Christ's image.

Romans 12:2 - "Do not conform to the pattern of this world, but be transformed by the renewing of your mind. Then you will be able to test and approve what God's will is—his good, pleasing and perfect will."

Transformation through grace stands at the heart of authentic Christianity—not merely behavioral modification but deep, internal renewal that progressively aligns our character with Christ's. This grace-driven change begins not with external rules but with internal renovation, as God's Spirit works to heal our wounds, reshape our thinking, redirect our desires, and reorient our priorities. When we embrace this transformative process, we experience freedom from both legalistic performance and permissive license, discovering instead the liberating joy of becoming who we were created to be.

Paul's instruction presents transformation as both a divine work and a human responsibility—God initiates and empowers the change, but we must actively participate through the "renewing of your mind." The Greek term for "transformed" (metamorphoō) suggests a profound, visible change comparable to a caterpillar becoming a butterfly, while the present tense indicates an ongoing process rather than a one-time event. The primary battleground for this transformation is our thought life, as we replace worldly patterns of thinking with biblical truth and eternal perspective. As we practice this mental renewal—through Scripture meditation, truth-based declarations, and community reinforcement—we develop self-awareness that recognizes when we're defaulting to old thought patterns or cultural assumptions rather than Kingdom perspectives. This awareness allows us to identify areas where transformation is needed and to cooperate intentionally with God's refining work. The promised result—discernment of God's will—reveals that transformation isn't just about personal spiritual growth but about aligning with divine purposes in the world, enabling us to recognize and respond to God's leading with greater clarity and confidence.

33. Embrace Your Uniqueness and Specialness

Celebrate the unique qualities and gifts God has given you, using them to glorify Him and serve others. Honoring your God-given uniqueness creates a powerful spiritual foundation that counters both pride and self-deprecation. When you deliberately recognize and celebrate your distinctive qualities and gifts as divine endowments—viewing them as sacred trusts rather than personal achievements or random attributes—you develop a healthier spiritual perspective on your individuality. This appreciative awareness gradually deepens your self-understanding, helping you recognize how your particular blend of strengths, experiences, and personality traits equips you for specific contributions to God's kingdom work. The habit of embracing your God-crafted specialness illuminates your particular calling more clearly, cultivating richer awareness of how your distinctive makeup serves as a unique expression of divine creativity and intention. Through faithful celebration of your God-designed uniqueness, your spiritual perception expands beyond conformity to a profound understanding of how your individual design fits purposefully within the larger body of Christ.

Psalm 139:14 - "I praise you because I am fearfully and wonderfully made; your works are wonderful, I know that full well."

Embracing our God-given uniqueness requires a delicate balance—acknowledging our distinctive design without either pride or false modesty. This acceptance recognizes that our specific combination of personality traits, natural abilities, spiritual gifts, and life experiences isn't accidental but intentional, crafted by a Creator who delights in diversity. When we celebrate rather than suppress our uniqueness, we honor the divine craftsmanship that formed us and position ourselves to fulfill the specific purposes for which we were designed.

David's poetic declaration reveals both awe at God's creative work and personal application of this truth to himself. The Hebrew terms "fearfully" (yare) and "wonderfully" (pala) convey being made with reverent care and distinguished excellence—suggesting that each human bears the marks of divine attention to detail. David's response to this revelation isn't embarrassment or deflection but wholehearted praise, recognizing that appreciating his unique design ultimately honors the Designer. As we practice this grateful acceptance of our uniqueness—neither hiding our gifts nor flaunting them, neither envying others' abilities nor diminishing our own—we develop self-awareness that recognizes both our strengths and limitations without shame. This awareness allows us to contribute our distinctive perspectives and abilities without either self-consciousness or self-importance, knowing that our uniqueness serves a divine purpose within the body of Christ. Through consistently embracing how God has made us, we experience the freedom to be authentically ourselves rather than exhausting ourselves through comparison or imitation, finding joy in expressing the particular aspects of God's character and creativity that He has embedded within us.

34. Define Priorities in Accordance with God

Align your life's priorities with God's commandments and purposes, ensuring that your actions reflect His will. God-aligned prioritization creates a transformative spiritual framework that fundamentally reorients your life's direction. When you deliberately filter your decisions and commitments through the lens of divine values—placing God's kingdom purposes above worldly measurements of success or fulfillment—you establish a powerful spiritual discipline that brings clarity amid competing demands. This intentional alignment gradually deepens your self-awareness, helping you recognize when cultural pressures or personal desires are subtly shifting your focus away from what truly matters in God's economy. The habit of divine-centered prioritization illuminates inconsistencies between your professed values and lived realities, cultivating richer awareness of how your day-to-day choices either strengthen or diminish your spiritual vitality. Through faithful ordering of your life according to God's priorities, your perception expands beyond immediate gratification to a profound understanding of how present decisions shape eternal outcomes, ultimately transforming your approach to time, relationships, and resources.

Matthew 6:33 - "But seek first his kingdom and his righteousness, and all these things will be given to you as well."

Priorities reveal what we truly value, not just what we claim to value. In a world of competing demands and endless options, defining priorities according to God's standards creates a framework for decision-making that brings clarity and purpose to daily choices. This alignment isn't about rigidly following religious rules but about organizing our lives around what matters most from an eternal perspective—relationship with God, growth in Christ-likeness, and participation in His redemptive work in the world.

Jesus' instruction to "seek first his kingdom" establishes a clear first priority that orders all others. This primary pursuit isn't one commitment among many but the central organizing principle for all of life. The word "seek" (zēteō) implies active, ongoing pursuit rather than passive interest, while "first" refers not just to chronological order but to preeminent importance. The promise attached to this priority—"all these things will be given to you as well"—addresses the anxiety about basic needs that Jesus had just discussed, assuring us that when we prioritize God's kingdom, He ensures our necessities are met. As we practice this God-centered prioritization—whether through intentional schedule choices, thoughtful resource allocation, or deliberate relationship investments—we develop self-awareness that recognizes when our stated priorities conflict with our actual behaviors. This awareness allows us to identify and address the gaps between what we say matters most and how we actually spend our time, energy, and resources. Through consistently aligning our priorities with divine values, we experience the freedom that comes from focusing on what truly matters, protected from both the tyranny of the urgent and the distraction of the trivial.

35. Have Personal and Professional Balance

Strive for a balanced life where personal faith and professional responsibilities complement each other, fostering overall well-being and effectiveness. The practice of faith-integrated balance creates a powerful spiritual framework that counters the fragmentation so common in our compartmentalized world. When you deliberately harmonize your faith commitments with professional responsibilities—seeing both as expressions of your spiritual identity rather than competing demands—you establish a more coherent and sustainable approach to life. This unified perspective gradually deepens your self-awareness, helping you recognize when imbalance in either direction is affecting your overall well-being and spiritual vitality. As you consistently work toward healthy integration of these domains, you'll develop heightened sensitivity to warning signs that indicate when professional ambition is eclipsing spiritual priorities or when religious activities are becoming disconnected from daily work. The habit of maintaining spiritual-professional balance illuminates how these areas can mutually reinforce rather than undermine each other, cultivating richer awareness of how God's presence can permeate both Sunday worship and Monday meetings. Through faithful attention to this holistic balance, your perception expands beyond artificial spiritual-secular divides to a profound understanding of how your entire life becomes sacred space when viewed through the lens of service to God.

Ecclesiastes 3:1 - "There is a time for everything, and a season for every activity under the heavens."

Balance in life doesn't mean equal time devoted to every area but rather appropriate attention given to each domain according to its importance and current season. This wisdom-guided equilibrium recognizes that different life phases require different allocations of our resources—some seasons demand intense professional focus, while others call for prioritizing family, health, or spiritual renewal. When we pursue thoughtful balance rather than rigid formulas, we honor God's design for rhythmic living, avoiding both workaholism that neglects relationships and disengagement that wastes opportunities.

Solomon's timeless observation about seasons provides a framework for understanding life's natural ebbs and flows. The Hebrew term for "time" (zeman) suggests not just chronological moments but appointed occasions—divinely orchestrated opportunities with purpose and meaning. This perspective liberates us from the pressure of trying to do everything simultaneously, acknowledging that legitimate activities have their proper moments. As we practice this balanced approach to life—making deliberate choices about where to focus in different seasons, establishing healthy boundaries between work and rest, and integrating faith principles into professional contexts—we develop self-awareness that recognizes signs of imbalance before they create damage. This awareness allows us to adjust our commitments, expectations, and habits when we notice areas of neglect or excess, preventing both burnout and stagnation. Through consistently pursuing wise balance rather than perfect equilibrium, we experience sustainable productivity and authentic relationship, demonstrating that God's design for human flourishing includes harmonious integration of all life dimensions rather than compartmentalization.

36. Follow the Callings and Leadings of God

Be attentive and obedient to God's directions in your life, trusting His guidance in every decision. When you deliberately cultivate sensitivity to God's guidance—recognizing His voice through scripture, prayer, wise counsel, and circumstances—you develop a dynamic relationship with divine direction rather than merely following static rules. This responsive obedience gradually deepens your self-awareness, helping you distinguish between God's authentic leadings and impulses driven by fear, pride, or cultural pressure. As you consistently respond to divine promptings with faithful action, you'll develop heightened discernment regarding God's unique communication patterns in your life, noticing the subtle internal nudges or external confirmations that often signal His direction. The habit of following God's callings illuminates your specific spiritual journey with greater clarity, cultivating richer awareness of how seemingly disconnected promptings often reveal a coherent divine narrative unfolding in your life. Through faithful attention to God's guidance, your spiritual perception expands beyond self-determined paths to a profound understanding of how surrendered obedience creates space for unexpected divine purposes that far exceed what you might have planned for yourself.

Proverbs 3:5-6 - "Trust in the Lord with all your heart and lean not on your own understanding; in all your ways submit to him, and he will make your paths straight."

Following God's leading requires both spiritual sensitivity to recognize His direction and courageous obedience to act upon it. This divine guidance seldom comes through dramatic supernatural events but more commonly through Scripture's wisdom, the Holy Spirit's gentle promptings, godly counsel, circumstantial doors opening or closing, and internal peace that surpasses understanding. When we develop the habit of seeking and following God's leading, our lives take on a purposeful trajectory that may not always make sense from worldly perspectives but ultimately proves perfectly aligned with divine wisdom.

Solomon's instructions establish both the attitude and the action needed to discern God's path. The command to "trust" (batach) conveys complete reliance and confidence rather than tentative hope, while "with all your heart" demands comprehensive commitment rather than partial allegiance. The warning against leaning on our own understanding acknowledges the limitation of human wisdom, which is often shortsighted and self-centered compared to God's eternal perspective. As we practice this submitted approach to life direction—consistently bringing decisions before God, seeking His wisdom above human advice, and choosing obedience even when the path seems unclear—we develop self-awareness that distinguishes between our preferences and God's leading. This awareness helps us recognize when we're resisting direction due to fear, comfort, or pride, enabling more consistent alignment with divine purposes. Through following God's leadings, even in small daily choices, we experience the promised "straight paths"—not absence of obstacles but clarity of direction and confidence that our journey, however winding it may appear, is unfolding according to divine design.

37. Exercise Lively Faith and Hope

Cultivate a vibrant and active faith, holding onto hope in God's promises, regardless of circumstances. The practice of cultivating active faith and resilient hope creates a powerful spiritual foundation that transcends circumstantial happiness. When you deliberately exercise your faith through consistent trust and expectant hope—especially during challenging seasons—you develop spiritual muscles that recognize God's faithfulness even when immediate evidence seems lacking. This hope-filled perspective gradually deepens your self-awareness, helping you identify when doubt or discouragement are undermining your spiritual vitality rather than merely reflecting emotional responses to difficulties. As you consistently choose to anchor yourself in God's promises instead of present realities, you'll develop heightened sensitivity to how your internal faith narrative shapes your perception of external circumstances. The habit of maintaining vibrant hope illuminates areas where pessimism or past disappointments have created spiritual blind spots, cultivating richer awareness of how your expectations often influence what you're able to perceive of God's activity in your life. Through faithful exercise of lively faith, your spiritual perception expands beyond what is immediately visible to a profound understanding of unseen realities, fundamentally transforming how you navigate life's uncertainties with confidence in God's unfailing character.

Hebrews 11:1 - "Now faith is confidence in what we hope for and assurance about what we do not see."

Lively faith transcends mere intellectual agreement with religious propositions to become a dynamic, animating force that shapes our decisions, sustains us in trials, and propels us toward God-honoring risks. This vibrant trust combines both backward-looking confidence based on God's proven faithfulness and forward-looking hope anchored in His unfailing promises. When we nurture this kind of active faith, it becomes not just a component of our spiritual life but its very engine, providing motivation and resilience that passive belief alone cannot sustain.

The writer of Hebrews provides not just a theological definition but a practical description of faith in action, using terms that emphasize its substantive reality. The Greek word for "confidence" (hypostasis) literally means "foundation" or "substance," while "assurance" (elegchos) suggests evidence that proves something's reality. Together, these terms present faith not as wishful thinking but as the means by which future promises and unseen realities become present certainties that influence current choices. As we practice this hope-filled, action-oriented faith—stepping out in obedience despite uncertainty, trusting God's character when circumstances seem contradictory, and basing decisions on biblical promises rather than visible probabilities—we develop self-awareness that recognizes when fear, doubt, or pragmatism is overriding our faith commitments. This awareness allows us to realign our thinking and choices with spiritual reality rather than temporary appearances. Through consistently exercising lively faith, we join the lineage of those described throughout Hebrews 11 who accomplished extraordinary things not because of exceptional human resources but because they lived as if God's promises were more real than present circumstances.

38. Lead and Influence as a Kingdom Ambassador

Represent the values and teachings of Christ in your interactions, influencing others positively as an ambassador for God's kingdom. The practice of intentional kingdom representation creates a transformative spiritual framework that elevates everyday interactions to sacred opportunities. When you deliberately embody Christ's values in your relationships and decisions—viewing yourself as heaven's ambassador rather than merely a private believer—you establish a powerful spiritual mindset that infuses ordinary moments with divine purpose. As you consistently embrace this role of spiritual influence, you'll develop heightened sensitivity to how your choices create ripple effects beyond your immediate circumstances, affecting how others perceive not just you but the God you serve. The habit of kingdom-minded leadership illuminates areas where cultural values may have subtly compromised your witness, developing greater awareness of how your life communicates certain truths about God even when you're not explicitly sharing your faith. Through faithful representation of divine values, your spiritual perception expands beyond personal piety to a profound understanding of how God uses your authentic witness as a vessel for His transformative presence in spaces where others might never encounter Him otherwise.

2 Corinthians 5:20 - "We are therefore Christ's ambassadors, as though God were making his appeal through us. We implore you on Christ's behalf: Be reconciled to God."

Kingdom ambassadorship transforms every interaction into an opportunity for divine representation, recognizing that we speak and act not merely as private individuals but as official representatives of Christ. This diplomatic role carries both tremendous privilege and weighty responsibility—we embody the message we proclaim, either enhancing or undermining its credibility through our attitudes and actions. When we embrace this ambassadorial identity, we approach relationships with intentionality, recognizing that our conduct may significantly shape others' perceptions of the King we represent.

Paul's powerful metaphor draws from the Roman diplomatic system, where ambassadors carried the full authority of the emperor they represented. The phrase "as though God were making his appeal through us" highlights the astounding reality that God chooses to work through human representatives rather than communicating exclusively through supernatural means. This divine partnership dignifies our role while emphasizing our dependence on the authority behind us. As we practice this conscious representation—aligning our words with biblical truth, demonstrating Christ-like character in challenging situations, and extending grace even when it's not reciprocated—we develop self-awareness that recognizes when our actions contradict our message. This awareness helps us identify areas where our ambassadorship needs refinement, prompting growth in consistency between our proclamation and our practice. Through consistently representing Christ's kingdom values in our spheres of influence, we participate in God's reconciling work, creating bridges rather than barriers for others to experience the transformative reality of relationship with Him.

39. Choose to Feel, Think, Speak, and Do like Jesus

Align your emotions, thoughts, words, and actions with those of Jesus, striving to emulate His example in daily life. When you deliberately calibrate your emotions, thought patterns, speech, and actions to reflect Jesus's example—responding with compassion rather than judgment, speaking truth in love, or choosing service over self-interest—you're engaging in comprehensive spiritual formation that affects every dimension of your being. The habit of patterning yourself after Jesus illuminates the gap between your current character and His perfect example, forming better awareness of how transformation begins in your inner landscape before manifesting in visible behavior. Through faithful attention to Christ's example across these four domains, your spiritual perception expands beyond compartmentalized faith to a profound understanding of how authentic discipleship integrates your entire being into a cohesive reflection of Jesus.

1 Peter 2:21 - "To this you were called, because Christ suffered for you, leaving you an example, that you should follow in his steps."

Christlikeness encompasses every dimension of our humanity—not just external behaviors but our emotional responses, thought patterns, verbal expressions, and tangible actions. This comprehensive transformation moves beyond selective imitation to whole-person alignment with Jesus' character and priorities. When we intentionally pattern our inner and outer lives after Christ's example, we experience not the restrictive conformity that stifles uniqueness but the liberating authenticity that fulfills our created purpose.

Peter's instruction reminds believers that following Christ's example isn't an optional spiritual upgrade but our fundamental calling as disciples. The Greek word for "example" (hypogrammos) originally referred to a writing pattern that students would trace to learn proper letter formation—suggesting precise, intentional imitation rather than vague inspiration. Significantly, this example is presented in the context of Christ's suffering, revealing that Christlikeness often costs us something—comfort, convenience, or personal advantage. As we practice this comprehensive emulation—responding to criticism with grace as Jesus did, prioritizing compassion over convenience, speaking truth with love, and serving without recognition—we develop self-awareness that recognizes the gap between Christ's pattern and our natural tendencies. This awareness helps us identify specific areas where transformation is needed, whether in emotional regulation, thought discipline, speech patterns, or behavioral choices. Through consistently choosing to align all dimensions of our lives with Jesus' example, we fulfill our identity as those being "conformed to the image of his Son" (Romans 8:29), becoming living illustrations of Christ's continuing presence in the world.

40. Be Selfless and Considerate

Prioritize the needs and well-being of others, showing selflessness and consideration in a manner that honors God. The practice of Christ-centered selflessness creates a beautiful paradox where giving yourself away leads to profound spiritual discovery. When you deliberately place others' needs before your own comfort—offering your time, attention, and resources without expectation of return—you participate in a divine rhythm that mirrors God's generous heart. This other-focused approach gradually illuminates hidden aspects of your character, revealing both the selfishness that naturally resists sacrifice and the capacity for love that reflects your Creator's image. As you consistently choose consideration over convenience, you'll experience unexpected moments of spiritual clarity where your perspective shifts from scarcity thinking to an abundance mindset that trusts in divine provision. The habit of selfless consideration creates sacred spaces for authentic connection that might otherwise be missed, cultivating deeper awareness of how God often works most powerfully through your willingness to be inconvenienced for another's benefit. Through faithful practice of this self-giving love, your spiritual vision expands beyond self-protection to a profound recognition of how your smallest acts of consideration can become living expressions of God's compassionate presence in a world desperate for genuine care.

Philippians 2:3-4 - "Do nothing out of selfish ambition or vain conceit. Rather, in humility value others above yourselves, not looking to your own interests but each of you to the interests of the others."

Selflessness counters our natural self-orientation with an others-focused approach to relationships and decisions. This quality doesn't eliminate appropriate self-care but rather challenges the default prioritization of personal comfort, convenience, and advancement over others' well-being. When we cultivate genuine consideration for others, we reflect the character of Christ, who consistently set aside His divine prerogatives to serve humanity's deepest needs.

Paul's instruction to the Philippians presents both what to avoid and what to embrace. The prohibited motivations—"selfish ambition" and "vain conceit"—address both action-oriented self-seeking and attitude-based pride. In their place, Paul calls for "humility" that perceives others' value and actively attends to their interests. This counter-cultural mindset doesn't come naturally but requires intentional practice and divine empowerment. As we develop this others-oriented perspective—whether by listening attentively without planning our response, considering how our choices affect those around us, or sacrificing preferences for others' benefit—we cultivate self-awareness that recognizes our reflexive self-focus. This awareness helps us identify when we're acting from selfish motives or prideful attitudes, allowing us to realign our priorities with Christ's example. Through consistently choosing consideration over convenience and service over self-interest, we participate in the profound kingdom inversion where greatness is measured by servanthood rather than status, and where the path to fulfillment paradoxically involves putting others first.

41. Hunger and Thirst for Justice and His Kingdom

Deeply desire and actively seek God's justice and the expansion of His kingdom on earth, reflecting His righteousness in your life. Kingdom-focused hunger creates a transformative spiritual lens that fundamentally reshapes what you value and pursue. When you deliberately cultivate a deep longing for God's justice—allowing His vision of righteousness to challenge your comfortable assumptions and redirect your ambitions—you develop spiritual appetites that align with divine priorities rather than cultural values. This holy discontent gradually deepens your self-awareness, helping you recognize areas where you've settled for personal peace while ignoring broader injustices that break God's heart. As you consistently nurture this sacred hunger, you'll develop heightened sensitivity to systemic inequities and individual suffering that might otherwise remain invisible to those satisfied with spiritual status quo. The habit of thirsting for God's kingdom illuminates how your everyday choices either advance or hinder His redemptive purposes, cultivating richer awareness of opportunities to embody divine justice through practical compassion and courageous advocacy. Through faithful cultivation of this kingdom hunger, your spiritual perception expands beyond personal blessing to a profound understanding of how your life can become a channel through which God's justice flows into broken places, fulfilling Christ's prayer for heaven's realities to manifest on earth.

Matthew 5:6 - "Blessed are those who hunger and thirst for righteousness, for they will be filled."

Spiritual hunger represents a compelling, visceral longing for God's righteousness—both personal holiness and societal justice. This passionate desire transcends casual interest or intellectual curiosity to become a driving force that shapes priorities, decisions, and actions. When we cultivate this deep yearning for God's kingdom values to be manifest in our lives and world, we align ourselves with His redemptive purposes, participating in His work of making all things new.

Jesus' beatitude employs intensely physical metaphors of hunger and thirst to describe this spiritual appetite, suggesting a need as basic and urgent as the body's requirement for food and water. The Greek terms used here indicate not mild hunger but intense craving, not slight thirst but desperate parching—conveying that righteousness should be pursued with the same urgency with which a starving person seeks food. The promise that such people "will be filled" guarantees divine satisfaction for this spiritual longing, though the passive construction indicates that this fulfillment comes from God rather than human achievement. As we nurture this kingdom hunger—through prayer for justice, study of God's standards, relationship with the marginalized, and intentional resistance to complacency—we develop self-awareness that recognizes when our appetites have shifted toward lesser pursuits. This awareness helps us identify areas where comfort, convenience, or cultural conformity have dulled our desire for God's righteousness, prompting renewed commitment to kingdom priorities. Through consistently cultivating this holy hunger, we experience both the divine satisfaction promised by Jesus and the joy of participating in God's work of restoration and redemption.

42. Emulate Christ's Character and Agape Love

Model your life after the character of Christ, showing unconditional, self-sacrificing love to everyone, just as He has shown to us. The practice of embodying Christ-like agape love creates a transformative spiritual pathway that elevates ordinary interactions to sacred encounters. When you deliberately choose to love others unconditionally—extending grace to the difficult, compassion to the wounded, and forgiveness to those who've hurt you—you participate in the most profound reflection of God's character possible in human experience. This sacrificial love gradually illuminates the deepest corners of your heart, revealing both your capacity for divine reflection and your need for continued grace. As you consistently practice loving beyond comfort or convenience, you'll discover moments of surprising spiritual clarity where your perspective shifts from self-protection to the liberating power of putting others first. The habit of Christ-modeled love creates opportunities for authentic connection that transcend religious performance, cultivating deeper awareness of how God often works most powerfully through your willingness to love when it costs you something. Through faithful emulation of this divine love, your spiritual vision expands beyond selective affection to a profound understanding of how your everyday acts of selfless love become living testimonies to the transformative power of the God who first loved you.

Ephesians 5:1-2 - "Follow God's example, therefore, as dearly loved children and walk in the way of love, just as Christ loved us and gave himself up for us as a fragrant offering and sacrifice to God."

Agape love distinguishes itself from other forms of affection by its sacrificial nature and unconditional commitment to others' highest good. This divine love doesn't depend on the worthiness of its object or fluctuate based on emotional response but remains steadfast regardless of reciprocation or merit. When we cultivate this Christ-like love, we participate in the most transformative force in the universe—the same love that moved God to send His Son and that empowered Jesus to endure the cross for humanity's redemption.

Paul's instruction frames this imitation of Christ not as burdensome obligation but as the natural response of "dearly loved children" who model themselves after their Father. The phrase "walk in the way of love" employs a Hebrew idiom that suggests consistent, daily practice rather than occasional emotional surges. The standard for this love is explicitly defined as Christ's self-giving sacrifice—a love demonstrated not primarily through sentiment but through costly action. As we practice this agape love—choosing patience when provoked, extending forgiveness when wounded, serving without recognition, and valuing others regardless of what they can offer in return—we develop self-awareness that recognizes the gap between Christ's perfect love and our natural tendencies. This awareness helps us identify situations where our love is conditional, self-protective, or performance-based, prompting greater dependence on the Holy Spirit's empowerment. Through consistently pursuing this Christlike character, we become living demonstrations of divine love in a world starved for authentic, unconditional acceptance, offering others a glimpse of the God who is Himself love.

43. Give Your Utmost for Him

Dedicate your best efforts in all you do as an offering to God, reflecting your gratitude and reverence for His gifts. Whole-hearted dedication transforms ordinary work into sacred offering that honors the Giver of all gifts. When you deliberately invest your fullest effort in each task—whether significant responsibilities or seemingly minor duties—you're engaging in a profound spiritual discipline that transcends mere productivity or performance metrics. This excellence-as-worship mindset gradually refines your self-awareness, helping you recognize when you're holding back parts of yourself that rightfully belong to God or giving Him leftover energy rather than your first fruits. As you consistently offer your best in each endeavor, you'll develop heightened sensitivity to the subtle ways your effort often reveals your true priorities and the condition of your heart toward God. The habit of giving your utmost illuminates areas where half-heartedness has become acceptable, cultivating richer awareness of how excellence offered from gratitude differs fundamentally from perfectionism driven by pride or fear. Through faithful stewardship of your talents and energy, your spiritual perception expands beyond compartmentalized devotion to a profound understanding of how every task becomes an opportunity to express love for the One who gave His very best for you.

Colossians 3:23-24 - *"Whatever you do, work at it with all your heart, as working for the Lord, not for human masters, since you know that you will receive an inheritance from the Lord as a reward. It is the Lord Christ you are serving."*

Giving our utmost transforms ordinary activities into sacred offerings when we recognize God as our primary audience and ultimate purpose. This perspective elevates the quality of our work not because of external recognition or material rewards but because excellence honors the God we serve. When we offer our best efforts as worship—whether in professional responsibilities, family relationships, church service, or personal development—we acknowledge that nothing is truly secular when done for divine purposes.

Paul's instruction to the Colossians addresses believers in various stations of life, including slaves who might have been tempted to offer minimal effort under compulsion. The phrase "with all your heart" translates a Greek expression that literally means "from the soul," suggesting wholehearted engagement rather than mere external compliance. The motivation for this excellence comes from recognizing that "it is the Lord Christ you are serving"—regardless of who signs the paycheck or evaluates the performance. As we practice this God-directed excellence—giving careful attention to details that others might overlook, maintaining integrity when shortcuts seem easier, and persisting in quality when recognition seems unlikely—we develop self-awareness that recognizes when we're slipping into mediocrity or performance driven primarily by human approval. This awareness helps us realign our motivation and effort with the standard of "as unto the Lord," recapturing the joy and purpose that come from serving Christ in everything. Through consistently offering our utmost, we create a compelling witness to the difference faith makes in daily life, demonstrating that belief in God transforms not just our eternal destination but our present approach to every responsibility.

44. Know Your Feelings: their Causes and Effects

Develop an awareness of your emotions, understanding what triggers them and how they affect your behavior and decisions. When you deliberately pay attention to your feelings—noticing their triggers, patterns, and influences on your decisions—you're engaging in a profound spiritual discipline that honors God's design of your complete humanity. This emotional attentiveness gradually deepens your self-understanding, helping you recognize when your reactions stem from past wounds rather than present realities, or when certain emotions consistently derail your spiritual intentions. The habit of emotional awareness creates space for more intentional choices rather than reactive behaviors, cultivating richer discernment of how God often speaks through your feelings rather than despite them. Through faithful attention to your emotional life, your spiritual perception expands beyond cognitive understanding to a more integrated awareness of how God works through your entire being—mind, body, and emotions—to guide you toward greater wholeness and authentic relationship with Him and others.

Psalm 139:23-24 - "Search me, God, and know my heart; test me and know my anxious thoughts. See if there is any offensive way in me, and lead me in the way everlasting."

Emotional self-awareness forms the foundation of spiritual and relational maturity—the ability to recognize, name, and understand our feelings rather than being controlled by them. This discernment involves identifying not just what we feel but why we feel it, recognizing how past experiences, core beliefs, unmet needs, and present circumstances interact to create our emotional responses. When we develop this understanding of our internal landscape, we gain freedom to respond thoughtfully rather than react impulsively, bringing our emotions under the Holy Spirit's influence rather than allowing them to drive our behavior.

David's prayer demonstrates a profound self-awareness combined with humble submission to divine examination. His request for God to "search me" and "know my heart" acknowledges both the importance of understanding our inner world and the reality that we often lack complete self-knowledge. The specific mention of "anxious thoughts" suggests attention to uncomfortable emotions rather than just positive ones, recognizing that our areas of fear and worry often reveal deeper beliefs and values. As we practice this emotional awareness—pausing to identify what we're feeling, reflecting on patterns in our emotional responses, and examining the beliefs behind our reactions—we develop self-understanding that recognizes emotional triggers before they control us. This awareness helps us distinguish between appropriate emotions that signal something important and disproportionate reactions rooted in past wounds or false beliefs. Through consistently seeking to know our feelings and their sources, we position ourselves for the transformation David seeks in the closing line of his prayer: to be led "in the way everlasting," with emotions serving as valuable indicators rather than unreliable masters.

45. Be Self-Disciplined, Controlled and in Command

Exercise self-discipline and control in your personal and spiritual life, mastering your impulses and behaviors to align with God's will. This intentional self-governance gradually deepens your self-awareness, helping you recognize when momentary urges threaten to override deeper values, or when lack of boundaries diminishes your spiritual effectiveness. As you consistently exercise holy restraint in thoughts, words, and actions, you'll develop heightened sensitivity to the subtle distinction between legalistic control and the fruit of Spirit-empowered self-discipline. The habit of spiritual self-mastery illuminates areas where undisciplined living has hindered your growth or witness, cultivating richer discernment of how seemingly small daily choices create momentum toward either spiritual vitality or stagnation. Through faithful stewardship of your impulses and behaviors, your spiritual perception expands beyond immediate gratification to a profound understanding of how disciplined living creates space for God's power to flow more fully through a life surrendered to His purposes.

2 Timothy 1:7 - "For God has not given us a spirit of fear, but of power and of love and of a sound mind."

Self-discipline represents the practical outworking of spiritual freedom—not rigid adherence to external rules but the internal mastery that enables us to choose God's best over momentary impulses. This control differs from mere willpower by acknowledging our dependence on the Holy Spirit's empowerment while still requiring our active participation. When we cultivate biblical self-discipline, we experience not the constriction of legalism but the liberation of living according to our new nature rather than being enslaved to fleeting desires or destructive habits.

Paul's assurance to Timothy identifies three divine gifts that contrast with fear and enable godly self-control. The "spirit of power" provides supernatural strength beyond our natural capabilities, "love" supplies the proper motivation for discipline, and a "sound mind" (sophronismos in Greek) conveys the concept of a disciplined, self-controlled mindset. Together, these gifts enable believers to master themselves without either harsh rigidity or undisciplined indulgence. As we practice this Spirit-empowered self-discipline—whether by establishing healthy boundaries, implementing spiritual disciplines, breaking destructive patterns, or cultivating positive habits—we develop self-awareness that recognizes our areas of vulnerability and strength. This awareness helps us implement appropriate safeguards in contexts where we're prone to temptation while building on areas where discipline has already taken root. Through consistently partnering with the Holy Spirit in this work of internal governance, we grow in character that increasingly reflects God's nature, demonstrating that true freedom isn't the absence of restraint but the presence of self-mastery that enables us to live according to our highest values.

46. Maintain a Constructive Attitude/Be Joyful

Create a positive and constructive outlook, choosing joy in all circumstances as a reflection of your faith. The intentional cultivation of spirit-anchored joy creates a transformative lens that fundamentally reorients how you experience life's circumstances. When you deliberately choose constructive perspectives amid challenges—seeing opportunities for growth rather than merely obstacles—you're practicing a profound spiritual discipline that transcends mere positive thinking. This joy-centered approach gradually deepens your self-awareness, helping you recognize when negative thought patterns have become habitual rather than reflective of divine truth, or when complaining has replaced gratitude as your default response. As you consistently exercise your spiritual authority over your attitudes, you'll develop heightened sensitivity to how your mental frameworks either invite or block awareness of God's presence in everyday moments. The habit of maintaining constructive joy illuminates the power you have to shape your experience through chosen perspective, cultivating richer discernment of how your attitude serves as either fertile or toxic soil for spiritual growth. Through faithful stewardship of your outlook, your spiritual perception expands beyond circumstantial reactions to a profound understanding of how choosing joy becomes not just a personal discipline but a powerful testimony to the sustaining grace available to those who trust in God's goodness regardless of external conditions.

Philippians 4:4 - "Rejoice in the Lord always. I will say it again: Rejoice!"

A constructive attitude shapes not just how we feel about circumstances but how we respond to them—seeing opportunities where others see only obstacles, finding lessons in difficulties, and focusing on solutions rather than dwelling on problems. This joyful outlook isn't naive optimism that denies reality but biblical realism that acknowledges challenges while viewing them through the lens of God's sovereignty and promises. When we cultivate this perspective, we demonstrate that our joy is anchored not in favorable circumstances but in an unchanging God whose character and commitment remain constant.

Paul's command to "rejoice in the Lord always" came from a prison cell, giving profound credibility to his instruction. The repetition—"I will say it again: Rejoice!"—emphasizes both the importance and the challenge of maintaining joy in difficult situations. The key phrase "in the Lord" reveals the source of sustainable joy—not our changing circumstances but our unchanging relationship with Christ. As we practice this constructive attitude—choosing gratitude over complaint, speaking life-giving words rather than criticism, and focusing on what God is doing even in challenging seasons—we develop self-awareness that recognizes when we're slipping into negativity, catastrophizing, or self-pity. This awareness helps us redirect our focus from present struggles to eternal perspective, from what's wrong to what's still right. Through consistently choosing biblical joy, we create an attractive witness to the difference faith makes, offering a compelling alternative to both toxic positivity and cynical pessimism—a joyful realism that acknowledges difficulties honestly while maintaining confident hope in God's faithfulness.

47. Learn, Grow, and Deliberately Improve

Embrace continuous learning and personal growth, intentionally seeking to better yourself in alignment with God's purpose. The sacred practice of intentional growth ignites a powerful spiritual momentum that transforms stagnation into holy progression. When you deliberately pursue learning as worship—seeing personal development not as self-improvement but as stewardship of divine potential—you participate in the profound spiritual discipline of becoming more fully who God created you to be. This growth mindset gradually illuminates your unique design, revealing both gifted areas ready for refinement and underdeveloped capacities waiting to be discovered. As you consistently invest in your development—whether through study, mentorship, or reflection on life lessons—you'll experience moments of beautiful clarity where new understanding creates expanded capacity for service and deeper spiritual perception. The habit of deliberate improvement creates a humble receptivity to God's shaping work, cultivating richer awareness of how your willingness to grow often becomes the very channel through which divine wisdom flows into your life. Through faithful commitment to learning, your spiritual vision expands beyond comfortable limitations to a profound recognition that your journey of growth becomes a living testimony to the God who continues His redemptive work in you day by day.

Proverbs 1:5 - "Let the wise listen and add to their learning, and let the discerning get guidance."

Deliberate growth recognizes that spiritual maturity doesn't happen automatically but requires intentional investment and lifelong learning. This commitment to development acknowledges that God's sanctifying work in our lives typically occurs through ordinary means—consistent study, humble reception of feedback, disciplined practice, and thoughtful reflection on experience. When we embrace this growth mindset, we move from passive consumers of spiritual content to active participants in our transformation, cooperating with the Holy Spirit's refining work.

Solomon's instruction reveals that wisdom doesn't eliminate the need for continued learning but rather increases the desire for it. The word "add" (yasaph) suggests ongoing accumulation—a lifelong process of building upon existing knowledge rather than a one-time achievement. The parallel reference to "guidance" highlights that growth doesn't happen in isolation but requires input from others who can provide perspective, correction, and direction. As we practice this deliberate improvement—whether through systematic Bible study, intentional skill development, honest self-evaluation, or strategic mentoring relationships—we develop self-awareness that recognizes both our growth areas and learning patterns. This awareness helps us identify which aspects of character or competence need focused attention and which learning approaches are most effective for our unique wiring. Through consistently pursuing growth with purpose and patience, we experience the paradoxical Christian reality that maturity increases rather than decreases our sense of dependence on God, as greater wisdom reveals both how much we've grown and how much growth remains possible.

48. Seek Feedforward Growth and Actualization

Focus on future-oriented feedback that helps you grow and actualize your potential, aligning your development with God's will. When you intentionally pursue growth-oriented feedback—inviting input focused not on past mistakes but on future potential—you engage in a profound spiritual discipline that honors God's ongoing work in your life. This forward-looking perspective gradually illuminates your unique calling, revealing both undeveloped gifts awaiting expression and specific growth edges where intentional development aligns with divine purposes. As you consistently welcome constructive guidance with humble receptivity, you'll experience breakthrough moments where others' insights become catalysts for spiritual leaps that might otherwise take years of solitary effort. The habit of seeking feedforward creates an acceleration of your growth journey, cultivating deeper awareness of how God often speaks prophetically through others' perspectives about your potential. Through faithful attention to this future-focused input, your spiritual vision expands beyond current limitations to a profound understanding of how your deliberate development becomes a living testimony to the God who calls you not just to be transformed but to participate actively in your own becoming.

Hebrews 12:11 - "No discipline seems pleasant at the time, but painful. Later on, however, it produces a harvest of righteousness and peace for those who have been trained by it."

Feedforward growth shifts our focus from past mistakes to future possibilities, emphasizing potential rather than problems. Unlike traditional feedback that often dwells on what went wrong, this future-oriented approach actively seeks input on how to improve, develop, and better align with God's purposes. When we cultivate this growth mindset, we become more receptive to guidance, correction, and challenging perspectives that might otherwise trigger defensiveness, recognizing them as valuable resources for our development rather than threats to our self-image.

The writer of Hebrews acknowledges the temporary discomfort of discipline while highlighting its lasting benefits. The Greek term for "discipline" (paideia) encompasses both correction and instruction—a comprehensive training process aimed at character formation rather than mere behavior modification. The metaphor of a "harvest" suggests that growth requires both time and proper conditions, with present discomfort yielding future flourishing. As we practice this actualization-focused approach—actively seeking constructive input, responding non-defensively to correction, and implementing specific growth strategies—we develop self-awareness that distinguishes between our current reality and our divine potential. This awareness helps us identify both the gap between who we are and who God is calling us to become, and the specific steps needed to navigate that distance. Through consistently embracing the temporary discomfort of growth processes, we position ourselves to experience the promised "harvest of righteousness and peace"—not just improved performance but transformed character that increasingly reflects God's nature and purposes.

49. Find Meaning and Purpose through Him

Discover your life's meaning and purpose through a relationship with God, understanding that your true fulfillment comes from aligning with His plans. Seeking purpose rooted in God transforms your life, grounding it in eternal significance instead of fleeting pleasures. By intentionally pursuing your calling through a close relationship with Him—understanding that true purpose stems from your connection with the Creator, not personal ambition—you embark on a deep spiritual journey beyond mere career goals. This God-centered quest gradually unveils your unique design, showing how your passions, talents, and experiences align with His redemptive work. Consistently seeking His guidance brings moments of profound clarity, revealing the purpose of seemingly random events within His larger plan. Finding meaning through this relationship beautifully integrates your identity and calling, fostering a deeper awareness that true fulfillment comes not from achievement but from who you become in faithful obedience. Aligning with God's purposes expands your spiritual vision beyond self-interest to a profound understanding of how your story gains its deepest meaning when intentionally woven into His grand narrative.

Jeremiah 29:11 - "For I know the plans I have for you," declares the LORD, "plans to prosper you and not to harm you, plans to give you hope and a future."

Meaning and purpose represent fundamental human needs that find their deepest fulfillment not in achievements, acquisitions, or accolades but in alignment with divine design. This God-centered purpose transcends the temporary satisfaction of self-focused ambitions to connect us with something larger than ourselves—the eternal purposes of the kingdom. When we discover our meaning through relationship with God, we experience the profound fulfillment that comes from operating according to our created design, utilizing our unique gifts and positioning for contributions that matter beyond our lifetime.

Jeremiah's prophetic message to Israel in exile offers assurance of God's good intentions even in difficult circumstances. The Hebrew word for "plans" (machashavah) suggests thoughtful, intentional designs rather than vague hopes—indicating that God has specific purposes uniquely suited to each person. The promised "prosperity" doesn't primarily indicate material wealth but comprehensive well-being, while the guaranteed "hope and future" addresses the deep human need for meaning beyond present difficulties. As we seek this divine purpose—through prayer for guidance, attention to how our gifts meet others' needs, wise counsel from those who know us well, and reflection on what brings deep rather than superficial satisfaction—we develop self-awareness that recognizes the difference between purpose-driven and merely productive activities. This awareness helps us distinguish between pursuits that simply fill our time and those that fulfill our calling, enabling wiser stewardship of our limited resources. Through consistently aligning with God's purposes, we experience not just personal fulfillment but the joy of participating in eternal significance, creating impact that extends far beyond our temporal existence.

50. Look for the Lord and His Will in Everything

In all aspects of life, seek to discern and follow God's will, understanding that His guidance leads to the best outcomes. Centering your discernment on God creates a transformative framework, illuminating every decision with sacred purpose. By deliberately seeking His guidance in all things, big and small, you engage in a profound spiritual discipline that values His wisdom above your own. This consistent seeking sharpens your spiritual perception, helping you see His hand in circumstances, scripture, counsel, and inner peace that often point to His direction. Faithfully aligning with His will brings moments of extraordinary clarity where complex situations resolve through insights beyond your natural understanding. The habit of seeking God's guidance in everything beautifully integrates faith and daily life, revealing how seemingly separate decisions form a coherent pattern through His purpose. Intentionally attuning to God's will expands your spiritual vision beyond the immediate, leading to a profound understanding that surrendering to His guidance—even when challenging—ultimately yields far better outcomes than self-direction.

Proverbs 3:6 - "In all your ways acknowledge Him, and He will make your paths straight."

Seeking God's will in everything transforms our approach to life from compartmentalized religion to comprehensive relationship—recognizing no division between "spiritual" and "secular" areas of life. This integrated perspective invites divine guidance into decisions both momentous and mundane, from career choices and relationship commitments to daily routines and leisure activities. When we cultivate this habit of seeking God in everything, we develop spiritual sensitivity that recognizes His guidance not just in dramatic interventions but in the subtle promptings, timely wisdom, and providential circumstances that shape our journey.

Solomon's instruction to "acknowledge Him in all your ways" employs the Hebrew word yada, which suggests intimate knowing and intentional inclusion rather than mere intellectual recognition. This comprehensive acknowledgment means inviting God's perspective into every dimension of life—our work and rest, our relationships and solitude, our public roles and private moments. The promised result—straight paths—doesn't guarantee absence of obstacles but provides assurance of divine direction and purposeful progress. As we practice this all-encompassing seeking—pausing for guidance before decisions, evaluating options through a biblical lens, and remaining attentive to the Holy Spirit's leading—we develop self-awareness that recognizes when we're attempting to navigate life through self-sufficiency rather than divine dependence. This awareness helps us identify areas we've kept outside God's influence, prompting more complete surrender to His lordship. Through consistently seeking God's will in everything, we experience the profound peace and confidence that come from knowing our paths, however winding they may appear, are being straightened by the One who sees the end from the beginning and works all things together for our good.

Conclusion: The Journey Continues

As we come to the end of these 50 ways to deepen your spiritual and self-awareness, remember that what you hold in your hands is not merely a collection of concepts but an invitation to a transformative journey. The path of presence and purpose is not a destination to be reached but a pilgrimage to be embraced—one step, one choice, one moment of awareness at a time.

For Church Leaders and Ministry Staff

You stand at a sacred intersection, called to both experience God's presence and guide others toward it. As you implement these principles in your own life and ministry, know that your authentic journey matters more than perfect execution. The congregation or team you shepherd doesn't need another polished performance but a fellow pilgrim who models what it means to seek God honestly. Your vulnerability in growth may be the most powerful ministry tool you possess, showing others that spiritual maturity isn't about having all the answers but about continuing to ask the questions that lead to deeper relationship with God.

For Parents Nurturing the Next Generation

The greatest spiritual legacy you can leave your children isn't perfect religious instruction but the living example of a faith that engages both heart and mind. As you practice these principles in your home, you're creating sacred space where young hearts can discover not just rules to follow but relationship to embrace. When your children witness you seeking God in both joys and struggles, acknowledging your emotions with honesty, and choosing growth even when it's uncomfortable, you're laying a foundation that can sustain them through life's inevitable challenges. Remember that in God's economy, no sincere effort to nurture faith is ever wasted—even when the fruit isn't immediately visible.

For Mental Health Professionals Integrating Faith

Your work stands at the beautiful convergence of theological truth and psychological insight, addressing both eternal souls and embodied minds. As you incorporate these principles into your practice, you participate in God's healing work in uniquely powerful ways. Never underestimate how your faithful presence—attentive, compassionate, and wisdom-guided—creates space for divine encounter in the midst of human suffering. The integration you model between spiritual awareness and emotional intelligence offers clients not just coping strategies but pathways to wholeness that honors their complete personhood as image-bearers of God.

For Those in Spiritual Transition or Faith Crisis

If you've found this book during a season of questioning, doubt, or spiritual dryness, know that your hunger for more authentic connection with God is itself a sign of His work in your life. These moments of disruption often precede the deepest growth, as comfortable certainties give way to more genuine faith. The very questions that feel threatening may be God's invitation to know Him beyond inherited assumptions or religious performance. As you implement even one or two of these principles that resonate with you, trust that the God who began this work of transformation will be faithful to complete it—not despite your questions but often through them.

For Small Group and Bible Study Leaders

The community you nurture provides essential soil for spiritual growth that cannot happen in isolation. As you guide others through these principles, remember that your primary task isn't curriculum completion but creating space where authentic transformation can occur. When group members feel safe enough to move beyond religious platitudes to share real struggles, questions, and victories, the Holy Spirit works in powerful ways. The relationships formed around these shared practices often become lifelines of support and accountability that sustain faith far beyond your formal gathering times.

Wherever you find yourself on the journey of spiritual awareness, remember that growth is neither linear nor uniform. There will be seasons of dramatic insight and seasons of quiet persistence, moments of profound connection and periods of apparent silence. Through it all, the constant reality is not your perfect implementation of these principles but God's perfect faithfulness to you.

The God who created you with both emotional and spiritual capacity is the same God who continues to draw you toward greater awareness of His presence and purpose. He delights not in your perfection but in your participation—your willingness to keep showing up, to maintain the conversation, to take the next step even when the full path isn't visible.

As you close these pages, may you carry with you the liberating truth that the Christian journey isn't about performing for a demanding deity but participating with a loving Father who initiates, sustains, and completes the good work He has begun in you. The practices of spiritual awareness aren't meant to earn His favor but to position you to receive what He already freely gives—His presence, which is our ultimate purpose.

The journey continues. And you never walk it alone.

With faith, hope, and love,

Ronnie Cunningham, EIQ2 EI Center

www.ingramcontent.com/pod-product-compliance
Lightning Source LLC
Chambersburg PA
CBHW081241020426
42331CB00013B/3257